T0413874

ZEN
and the art of
PEACEFUL LIVING

DR. DAVID DOLEZAL

CONTENTS

INTRODUCTION

For anyone who has ever stared down at the lifeless body of a loved one, I understand. As the doctor described what he believed to be the inevitable next steps, an overwhelming sorrow welled up within me from a place more profound than I had ever known before, causing tears to flow in rivers down my expressionless face. I felt I lost my father, my rock, and my friend forever, and I had no idea where he had gone. Emotionally alone and in a kind of shock from the death to the burial, I tried to play the part of the excellent son while surrounded by well-wishing family, friends, and strangers who tried their best to help me through the ordeal. Some told me that he was in a better place, some gave me condolences, some wanted to comfort me with hugs, and some awkwardly tried to lighten up the moment with what they thought was comic relief.

I remember the church service before the burial. The location was in a plain building that looked as if it could have been built in the nineteen seventies in a tiny town in Montana. It was no different than the kind of hall where veterans of foreign wars meet to drink beer, tell tall stories, and compare old wounds. The inside was also plain and unremarkable. There were numerous wooden benches on either side with a wide walkway down the middle. There were flower arrangements at the entry and a large wooden casket in front of a podium that the priest would use to deliver the sermon. Above and behind the podium was a nearly life-size carving of Jesus Christ nailed to a cross. My father had many family members and friends in attendance, many of whom I'd never met or hadn't seen in years, all talking quietly as they waited for the priest to begin. I recall my grandmother coming near and kissing me on my lips as I wondered what it must be like for her to have outlived her son. As the priest began a sermon that I cannot recollect, I looked up at the statue of Christ and, in a last-ditch effort to gain some control, promised Jesus quietly that he had better help my father get into heaven, or I would spend eternity making him pay for the error. I was negotiating with a statue. As I left the burial site, I drove away and wept. The tears became so blinding that driving became impossible, and I had to pull over. At that moment, on the side of the road, I paused, and I wondered who the tears were for. Were they for my father, or were they for me?

For months on end, I tried to hide my sorrow. I couldn't understand the point anymore. I would go to work without ambition, and at the end of the day, I would pour as many stiff drinks as was necessary to get a decent night's sleep. I started traveling to far-off exotic locations, going on wild adventures, getting crazy with friends, and looking for anything that would help me make sense of it all. In the water, halfway across the planet, I would look out over the ocean where the sky touches the sea and wonder if my father lay far beyond that. I began to wonder where he might have gone. I had no idea.

As a child and young man, I was invincible and had no reason to worry about such things. The more I wondered, the more I realized that I had simply taken everyone's word for the answers to life's most profound questions. As much as they loved me, my father, mother, family, and friends never really shared their knowledge or opinions. I realized I had gained most of my knowledge from Christmas specials that played on television each year during December and a class at the catholic church I attended from first through sixth grade called CCD. I had read some excerpts from the bible from time to time, but the church's translations and explanations of the text seemed unbelievable at best and crazy at worst. I mean, really, who actually understood the meaning of the holy trinity? That is why they called it the supreme mystery, because it remained a mystery to them, and they could never explain it. Going to church and listening to the priest felt like going to an auto mechanic who couldn't simply describe the problem with the car's engine. I recalled that all of it seemed like complete nonsense, and after I became a teenager, I never went back to church. But now, I wondered.

It was then that I decided to find out for myself. Instead of accepting the church's unintelligible doctrine or translations from family, friends, and strangers who had read the bible, I would read the book for myself. For that matter, I would read as many books as it took to get to the answer. I embarked on a ten-year reading binge in my spare time. I read everything I could get my hands on. I read over 40 books from all over the world, including The Torah, The Talmud, The Sacred Paths, The Christian bible, The Quran, The Book of Enoch, Watering the Soul, The Book of Mormon, The Holy Mother, Tao Te Ching, The teaching of Buddha, The Kebra Nagast, The complete Mahabharata, The Ashtavakra Samhita, The complete works of Vivekananda, and The Analects of Confucius. Of the many

Upanishads available, I read: The Katha, The Isha, The Prasna, The Mundaka, The Mandukya, The Taittiria, The Aiterya, The Chandogya, The brihadaranyaka, The Kaivalya, and the Svetasvatara.

As I read these books over the years, I slowly noticed that each author appeared to tailor their text for their listeners at the time of their production, and despite this, each book had very similar truths hidden within them. It was as if you imagined you were looking at a bucket, a cup, a pitcher, a lake, and a saucer filled with pure water. Each vessel is different, but they all carry the same water of truth within them. By the time I got around to the Gospel of Thomas ten years later, I not only knew where my father was, but when I read the first ten of 114 sayings of Jesus Christ, I could easily understand their meaning. As I read the sayings of Jesus further, I slowly realized that the knowledge I gained by reading these various texts must have been similar to the knowledge Jesus gained by reading the various texts available to him in Jerusalem during his lifetime.

That is when it struck me. Jesus Christ was Jewish, but he wasn't from the tribe of Levi. From the Hebrew Torah, I recalled God saying very clearly that the only Jews that could be Rabbis were the Jews from the tribe of Levi. Jesus' father, Joseph, was from the tribe of David, which meant that Jesus could never be a Rabbi. So, even though Jesus showed real promise and was a brilliant student of the Torah, he was destined to be a carpenter's apprentice like his father once he turned 13. After Jesus came of age, Jesus likely worked with his father on varying projects in a very modern city for the period. The world under Roman control had plumbing, sanitation, roads, education, and much more. The Roman Empire at its height was likely as magnificent as the United States was at its height in the late twentieth century. Rome improved all of the nations that it conquered. Proof of this can be seen in the British Isles. Rome conquered England in the south but never conquered Scotland to the north. After decades of subordination and after Romes's fall, England was much more advanced than Scotland and remained that way for hundreds of years. Under Roman occupation on the opposite side of Roman territory to the east, Judea faired no differently. While the Jews may have resented their subjugation, they benefitted from Romes's modern advancements.

Knowledge from across the world and books of all varieties carried by wealthy traders must have been available in the area where Jesus worked and lived. In the same manner that he debated in front of the temple as a child, it is easy to imagine that he did the same at various other temples during his leisure time. Remember, back then, there were no movies, televisions, tick-tock, or YouTube shows to occupy the mind of a brilliant young carpenter when he was off of work.

As I reflected on the texts I had read, I realized that the sayings of Jesus Christ were a reflection of the theological and philosophical knowledge he had gained came from the many books he'd read and from the many people from different faiths and philosophies that he came across and debated while at rest from his professional career in carpentry. Jesus only became a teacher and an activist once he became unshakable in his new philosophy at the ripe old age of thirty-one. With his breadth of newfound knowledge, this brilliant young man became like a prophet to his brethren because he discovered an entirely new way to interpret the meaning of the Torah and shared it fearlessly. The best way I can describe it is a kind of

Judeo-Vedantic fusion that led to his Christian philosophy, a new way of looking at the same old Torah and discovering hidden truths within the text from an entirely new perspective.

Around the same time that I came to this realization, I also became blessed with two beautiful children, a son and a daughter. I often refer to them as angels because when I looked into their eyes for the first time, I felt I could see the angel deep within them. As my attention turned towards them, I wanted what every decent father wants for their children: a beautiful life experience filled with health, love, happiness, and peace.

I wanted to help the children proactively in any way possible, including educating them on understanding the game of life and enjoying its beauty peacefully. I wanted to share the knowledge I gained from my studies that helped me find my father, myself, the beauty in life, and genuine peace. To do that, among other things, I began to write short stories that reflected my new knowledge. As the children grew from day to day, there were moments when they presented me with learning opportunities. In those moments, when the children would ask about a specific subject, I would intellectually look back on my years of study and meditation and share what I had come to understand with them. After I shared my answer to the children's question, I wrote down the thoughts I shared with them in greater depth, so if the children ever got older and, like me, "really needed to know," they wouldn't have to spend ten years on their own looking for the same answers that I had already discovered. Because they were young, I made a special effort to keep the stories as simple as possible and less than five pages per story so that they could get more or less straight to the point of each subject. I even unraveled and wrote down the logical meaning behind the supreme mystery of the Holy Trinity for them within those parameters.

That is how this book came into being. As of this writing, I am celebrating 60 years of living. My children have become successful adults, and my wife and I feel it is time to share these stories with you and your loved ones. Ten years of reading and eleven years of writing did not only produce what I humbly believe is the best way to understand the meaning of the sayings of Jesus Christ. It also made a new way to see the beauty in the world around you and the knowledge that will help you achieve genuine peace and contentment. In my best estimation, this book rediscovers a previously lost point of view that I believe even Jesus would be proud of, based on common sense and practical philosophy rather than blind acceptance of faith and miracles. It provides a paradigm shift that will bring you back to your old bible with a fresh new perspective.

THE WORLD IS AN ILLUSION

Long ago, when people used to look out upon the desert, some believed they could see water off in the distance. But now, most know that is only an illusion. To some, the word "Illusion" might be interpreted to suggest that the world they believe they see around them is not real at all. But that interpretation is wrong. An illusion is not something that doesn't exist. An illusion is something that does exist but is not what it appears to be. The word "Illusion" can also mean "The world human that beings see all around them is an appearance that human beings are currently too ignorant to understand fully." It does not mean they can't understand; it simply means their current level of knowledge has left them unable to understand completely at this moment in time.

Humanity's current level of ignorance could be likened to a very young child who does not understand the concept of numbers. Not because the child has a low IQ or needs to try harder. It is simply because the child is young. As the child grows, the child will eventually learn numbers and then may subsequently learn more abstract formulas. Time and study were necessary for the child to gain experience and knowledge because the information was always there. It is similar to the perceived physical world. Because human beings' knowledge is limited, they cannot yet understand its full complexity. That does not mean that the answers are not there. The answers have always been there.

For example, hundreds of years ago, human beings mistakenly believed the world was flat throughout the civilized Western world. Kings and queens, the most significant intellectual minds of the time, the rich and the poor, believed the earth was flat. That is until someone sitting on a beach observed a ship with large sails as it sailed away from land and straight out into the ocean. That person noticed that the vessel and its large sails did not only get smaller, but the ship also appeared to sink into the ocean until, after the ship traveled far enough away, it appeared to sink entirely into the ocean. When the boat returned unscathed, the man sitting on the beach realized that the ship hadn't sunk at all. The boat appeared to be sinking because it was sailing around a circular world. A few courageous sailors proved him right by circumnavigating the globe, and suddenly, human beings throughout the entire Western world came to understand that the Earth was round. In this way, their newly acquired knowledge replaced the illusion that had lasted for thousands of years. The truth was always there. They were simply ignorant of the truth until their knowledge had sufficiently developed.

Around the same time, most humans believed that the Earth was the center of the universe and that the sun, moon, and stars all revolved around it. Those ancient people firmly believed that the sun rose and set around the planet Earth every day because it looked that way from where they were standing. With their limited level of knowledge at the time, it made perfect sense. Eventually, as humanity studied and grew more knowledgeable, they realized that the sun was the center of our tiny solar system and that the Earth's rotation made the sun appear to rise and set around the planet. Suddenly, as their ignorance was wiped away, so was the illusion.

The "The illusory world," is a world that appears to be what it is not. This is not because human beings don't possess the capacity to understand it but because, with their current level of knowledge, they remain ignorant of the fullness of reality. In a similar way to those who lived long ago, humanity's current ignorance causes them to see the world as they want to rather than as it actually is.

Intellectually imagine that you are looking at a table. The table looks very much like a table. But if you can look at the table more closely, you will see that it is not only a table. It is also molecules. And if you look more closely than that, you will see that it is not only molecules but also atoms. Each atom, a solar system of sorts, composed almost entirely of space. Looking more closely, you will see they are also subatomic particles. The more closely you look at the table, the more you will realize it is not what you believed it was at first glance. In this way, the previously solid-looking table can eventually be seen as material energy.

Now, look at the same imaginary table differently. In that case, you will realize that the image you see as a table is only light waves reflecting off an object and into your eyes. As the light waves enter your eyes, the rods and cones within your eyes create an image of a table. Those rods and cones then activate the optic nerves, special living cells that relay electrochemical impulses to your brain cells. Each of these brain cells, these neurons, these individual life forms, then store and maintain the information collected by your body to be used by you, as and when needed. Once the brain cells receive the information, the mind will begin to integrate the information with all of the prior information received and contained in all the other neurons. This integration occurs so that the mind can help the person formulate a best guess about what is happening in the perceived external world. So, what you believe is a table you are seeing from this perspective is merely the reception of electrochemical impulses relayed by living organisms called sense organs to other living organisms called brain cells, wholly cut off from the very external world you are attempting to understand.

What a person concludes they are receiving from the external world represents nothing more than a kind of contact from some perceived external force to the cells of the perceived physical eyes. This perceived contact initiates a reaction within the human brain, and the mind projects an image when there is sufficient physiologic reaction. This interaction does not represent reality; it merely represents the mind as the perceived contact has altered it. So, what you have been thinking is the external world, which remains entirely unknown, is, in reality, only a perceived external world plus the mind.

What you are looking at might not be a table at all. The only reason you believe it is a table is that your body, with its limited sense organs and your limited understanding, reacted to a stimulus and then projected an image within the mind that you chose to accept as a table. In actuality, the table represents nothing more than a sort of controlled hallucination brought on by your mind after an impulse was believed to have been received by your sense organs. It is common knowledge that limb amputations can result in abnormal body awareness. Many human beings who have undergone amputation have reported phantom limb sensation as a sensory experience that they perceived originated from a missing body part. You believe the table is not a hallucination because, throughout your life, you have been taught that it is a table, and other human beings agree with your idea. It is your shared belief in the concept that makes it a table. You did not believe you felt or saw atoms, the almost one hundred percent space within the composition of the table, or the subatomic particles. If you had, other human beings would likely have said you were crazy. In this case, you chose, with your limited understanding, limited information, and your agreement with others, to see the table as a solid place to put your books. That did not represent the fullness of reality; it represented your best guess as to what reality was.

When the mind continually attempts to create a best guess about an external universe that it is thus far incapable of fully understanding, it inevitably causes the mind to organize incorrectly and further misunderstand the information received. The result is that human beings end up continually arranging and re-arranging the external perceived physical world into concepts they can understand and manage rather than as it truly is. This is the mirror they look upon when they incorrectly believe they are looking out at the real world around them. Their mind injects their past misunderstanding and beliefs into the limited information they believe they are receiving from the neurons. This interference by the mind and the resultant misunderstanding creates a false and illusory world.

Before the invention of home movies, everyone had to go to the theatre to see a moving picture. All the people who paid for admission walked inside a large, well-lit theatre room with hundreds of seats, all in rows facing a movie screen where the person in the back of the theater operating the projector would play the movie. The patrons could see every aspect of the theatre as they entered, and all the other people around them who were also looking for seats to sit in while watching the movie. They could easily see the reality all around them.

Then, at a specific time, once everyone was seated, the movie theatre personnel would turn off the lights and turn on the movie projector. A moving picture magically appeared on the screen to be viewed by all attendees. Within moments in the darkness, all attendees forgot about their prior reality and became distracted by the movie playing on the screen instead. The movie became their new reality. The sad images made them cry, the funny images made them laugh, and the frightening images raised the hairs on their arms. If the movie was entertaining or engaging enough for the people sitting in the darkness, it became their reality for approximately two hours, and the real world that existed when they entered was utterly forgotten.

It is the same with the perceived external physical world all around you. When humans are born, they immediately become distracted by the perceived physical world. Like the people at the movie theatre, they begin to believe the information they experience through their limited senses of taste, touch, smell, hearing, and sight is the totality of reality. They cannot recall where they came from before birth and become transfixed on the material energy of the perceived physical world and its effects on their limited sense organs.

Imagine that you just purchased a new video game at the store. As soon as you get home, you excitedly plug one cable from the game into a power source, one from the game into the television, and turn the power on. Almost instantly, the video game becomes visible on the screen, and the graphics are amazing. You quickly go through the instructions for playing the game and happily play the game for hours. You do not know who designed or built the game. You do not know who programmed the game. You do not understand how the electricity runs from the wall to the game. You do not understand how the hardware works or how the software works. You only know that the game has impressive graphics, and with enough time and effort, you will likely be able to master the game. You enjoy the game without understanding the fullness of the reality of the game. The perceived physical world is very much like the video game. You don't know who created the game, who or what programmed the game, etc. You live in an illusory world, not because the perceived physical world is not real, but because you cannot comprehend the fullness of reality. It is your limitations that force you to see the world as you want to rather than as the world actually is.

When people long ago used to look out upon the desert, some believed they could see water off in the distance. But now, most know that it is only an illusion. It is merely the difference in air density near the hot ground and the cooler air above, causing the air to act like a lens, sending an image of the blue sky toward the viewer and giving the appearance of water. Those earlier people with limited knowledge chose to see it as they wanted to see it rather than as it was. This reveals that people with a lower level of knowledge will believe the world they see around them and everything in it exists and really is experienced. However, those with a higher level of knowledge understand that the world they believe they are experiencing is, in reality, only an illusory projection created by them.

And how does one overcome this illusion? Knowledge. Studying and focusing enough on any subject you desire until you are intellectually able to break the chains of that specific illusion. Studying like the man on the beach who watched the ship heading outward to sea. His focus on that ship over time, combined with an open mind, led him to discover that the world was round, thus freeing himself from that illusion with his newly acquired knowledge. As you study and learn, your mind may begin to sort through its prior ideas and attempt to convince you to cling to them rather than consider a different point of view. Because of your firmly held prior beliefs, it may be difficult to accept new information without your mind trying to convince you to reject it. This moment is when meditation becomes essential. It's not the kind of meditation where you sit on a mountaintop with your legs crossed over a lion's skin, trying to make the world disappear. It's the kind of meditation that follows reading a book like this, watching a lecture, or thinking about what you saw a boat do earlier in the morning. This kind of meditation requires the mind to be open to new and different information, ensure the proper time is taken to intellectually review and think about the newly received information, and maybe even intellectually imagine the information from a different point of view. Over time, your newly acquired knowledge will gently and naturally move you closer to the truth. And don't worry about how long it takes; you will soon learn that time is also an illusion.

GOD IS ALL

The vast majority of human beings believe in some form of God, even those who profess there is no God. Those who say they do not believe in God will likely confess at some point, even if their idea of "God" doesn't exist; there is a shared and imagined idea of God that their religious neighbors believe in that does exist. These atheists will often begrudgingly accept that God, in that respect, can be seen as a sort of shared imagination or hallucination by different religious groups, in a similar way that some children believe in fictional characters like Santa Claus. In this regard, God is an imagined amalgam of sorts, whereby the different religions ascribe certain characteristics that align with their current idea of physical, moral, and spiritual perfection. Then, the majority of those within each religious group agree that the words of this amalgam, always given to an intermediary, are perfect, without flaw, and are the only truth; therefore, they must be dutifully obeyed.

To avoid falling into the quagmire of either of the previously mentioned groups, we will look at the concept of God from a slightly different perspective. For clarity, I will reframe the intellectual point of view and describe the word "God" as a term that includes all that is primordial, infinite, and without limiting attributes. In this sense, "God" will include everything known and unknown, manifest and unmanifest forever, including all energies and awareness itself. Under these conditions, some would desire to substitute this use of the word "God" with the word "NATURE." This substitution is impossible because the word "God" in this discussion is intended to express that which is infinite and without limit. "NATURE," or "the objective universe," represents only a fractional aspect of that greater reality.

In this respect, God is imminent, a part of, permeating, and beyond all objects, space, and time. God is the subject of all reality and thus is beyond speech and concepts. In this context, the word "God" cannot be adequately described, for any description would have to reduce God to something else. This "God" is everything known and unknown. This "God" is below, above, behind, before, to the right, and the left of you. This God is all of this, including your physical form.

An ancient text from the East called the Chandogya Upanishad helps to illustrate this idea of God being the primordial, infinite subject of all reality without limiting attributes. In the text, there is a dialogue between a sage and his son, Shvetaketu, who had just returned home after finishing his education elsewhere. To assess the son's education level, the sage asked Shvetaketu, "What is that knowledge by which everything becomes known?" They then used the reality of a clay pot to answer the question. To summarize their conversation more modernly, we will imagine looking at a bottle instead. At first glance, the bottle only appears to be an ordinary bottle. But if you look more carefully, you will notice that the bottle is composed of plastic. From that new perspective, you can see the ordinary bottle, but you will also see that the bottle is composed entirely of plastic. From that perspective, you can now see two things. You can see plastic and the bottle. If you look even more carefully than that, you will suddenly realize that the bottle is, in reality, only plastic. Plastic is the basic substance of the entire bottle. If someone melted down the bottle, there would only be a lump of plastic.

So, the object that you first saw only as a bottle, on closer observation, is now understood to be plastic alone, and what you initially thought was a bottle is merely the name and form that the plastic assumed. It is only because of plastic that the name and form of the bottle even exists. From that perspective, you will see that plastic is the actual reality. The plastic could have taken the form of a cup, a pitcher, a phone case, an artificial plant, clothing, a car bumper, a toy, or hundreds of thousands of different forms. Regardless of the plastic's form, its basic substance would still be plastic.

It is the same with God. It was said in the beginning that everything in existence was issued forth from God. Therefore, every "Thing" is from God, of God, and in God. So, like plastic, "God" can now be seen as the basic substance of the infinite universe, the one actual reality, and everything in the perceived physical universe is simply the endless number of names and forms that "God" assumes. Like gold that can be melted into a ring, re-melted into a necklace, and re-melted again into a bracelet while remaining gold, God is the basic substance of every name and form in the perceived physical universe.

Imagine that you are looking at a table. At first glance, the table appears very much like a table. But if you can look at the table more closely, you will see that it is not only a table but also molecules. And if you can look more closely than that, you will notice that it is not only molecules but also atoms. Each atom, its own solar system, composed almost entirely of space. If you can look even more closely, you will see subatomic particles. If you look even more closely than that, you will see that all matter can be reduced to tiny, almost transcendental strands of stuff, finer than the finest ether, that some modern physicists call superstrings, existing within the subatomic quantum field, that are acted upon by something that is as of yet unknown to science. That unknown something, that basic substance, is also God.

Those who say there is no God cannot explain the existence of the infinite material universe. If there were no one God, where did the material of the perceived physical universe come from? You can't create nothing from nothing. Without something greater than the infinite material universe, like a God existing as the infinite manifest and unmanifest, one would still need materials at least as big as the perceived infinite universe to start the Big Bang and bring the universe into existence. Where would the materials come from? And wouldn't you need at least two materials, like a lot of gasoline and an incredibly large lighter? Then, you would still be stuck with even more questions, like where they came from and which came first.

Although the world's different religions have varying narratives designed to fit their listeners' cultural norms and intellectual abilities at the time of their production, they have some interesting similarities in their stories of how the known universe was projected into being.

According to ancient Christians, the energy that manifested the Perceived physical universe from the subatomic quantum field is an unknown vibratory energy some call the word of God. The Christian disciple John wrote in his book, "In the beginning was the word, and the word was with God, and the word was God." Ancient Hindus support the Apostle John's statement by claiming "AUM" is the vibration that brings all things into manifestation. It represents the sacred sound, a sonic representation that is the essence of the supreme absolute, consciousness, and the cosmic world.

Since nothing can come from nothing, the perceived physical universe must have come from something. This something is the infinite, omnipresent reality that existed before what this generation of humanity calls creation. This God, this basic substance of everything, is primary to and simultaneously exists as all energies and matter from within the quantum field, manifesting itself as the perceived infinite universe. If you can imagine a slow-moving river that has little swirls or eddies within it that swirl for a time, stop swirling for a time, and then begin swirling again, you can imagine the perceived infinite universe as it comes into being, out of being, back into being and so on, forever. Instead of water in a river, consider it an infinitely flowing subatomic quantum field that manifests itself into matter and energy. This material energy is what you perceive as the infinite number of names and forms in the perceived physical world all around you, including the table.

A renowned theoretical physicist from the United States of America named John Hagelin, in his February 2015 lecture in New Deli, India, on "The Science of Technology and the Unified Field," revealed that the origin story found an ancient Indian book called the Rig Veda (Science Veda) written in 1500 BCE had scientific merit. He showed in his lecture, "One string in the quantum field is much like a guitar string and exists far removed from the perceived material world, almost as a transcendental thing, that has eight independent ranges of motion or resonant frequencies when acted upon. In the process of creating creation, the string undergoes a metamorphosis, a transformation, several of them. This superstring that lives in ten dimensions goes on to become a bosonic string that lives in 26 dimensions. Because the bosonic string exists in 26 dimensions, it has 24 vibrational states or frequencies. That is not the end. That bosonic string transforms itself again into what is called a pre-fermionic string that has 64 vibrational degrees of freedom, and finally, through a somewhat more complicated mechanism, in the last stage of transformation, the fermionic stage gives rise to a 192-fold vibrational structure through space-time super-compactification in preparation to create the material universe. One hundred ninety-two tones or sounds is the unified field reverberating within itself." Dr Hagelin continues, "If you compare that structure to the Rig Veda, which is described as the blueprint of the universe by Dr. Nader, the template on which the universe was structured, you see a very similar structure. You see that the Rig Veda elaborates on itself. The first eight syllables in the first sentence of the Rig Veda match the formula for one superstring. The next sentence has 24 syllables; the next sentence has 64 syllables, and the next sentence has 192 syllables as a sequential unfolding of unity through a precise sequence. The universe itself is a commentary on the Veda. The Veda unfolds from 8 to 24, to 64, to 192 as different packages of wholeness. Each representing the totality of knowledge."

Evidence supporting Dr Hagelin's theory can be found in the ancient "Hebrew Torah, " known as the "Old Testament." Its opening sentence states, "In the beginning, God created (projected) the heavens and the earth." And how was the universe created according to this ancient text? The third sentence states, "And God said…." These ancient texts from across the world agree that this God is the one true reality, primary to, imminent, a part of, permeating, and beyond all objects, space, and time. This God is primary to everything, with aspects of itself moving from an undifferentiated state to a differentiated state, appearing as the infinite perceived universe. From cause to effect, from effect to cause, again and again forever, God is the basic substance of everything.

Now, let's look at the same opening sentence of the Hebrew Torah from a slightly different angle. In the beginning can be considered time, God can be considered causal energy, created can be considered action, heaven can be considered space, and earth can be considered matter. According to this ancient Hebrew statement, everything necessary in physics for a perceived material universe to exist already existed. God and the perceived infinite universe are the same thing, just in different forms. God is the causal state, and the infinite perceived universe is the material state.

Imagine that I took some sand and heated it. That would be the very thing needed to create a glass bottle. But before I heated the sand, the sand would only be sand. With heat, it would become a bottle. The cause of sand and heat become the effect of the bottle. And what would happen if I smashed the bottle with a great stone again and again? The bottle would go back to its causal state of sand and heat. Similarly, God has always existed, and the universe is the effect. If you can intellectually imagine a kind of material energy so sub-atomically fine that it would be even finer than the strings that scientists discovered to exist in the subatomic quantum field, then you are getting closer to imagining the causal state of God.

Now imagine that infinitely fine energy acting upon the sub-atomic strings, causing them to vibrate until they begin to merge. They continue to merge until they become the matter around you. You will be getting closer to understanding the effect of God, which is called the perceived material universe. God did not create the per-ceived infinite universe; God projected it into being. God is the basic substance. God is imminent, a part of, permeating, and beyond all objects, space, and time. God is the subject of all reality and thus is beyond speech and concepts. God in this context cannot be ade-quately described, for any description would have to reduce God to something else.

So, while it may agitate some to think that God is thought of and worshipped in many different forms, such as the form of a man or an object, those who can see God from the perspective I've presented understand everything is in God, of God and from God; thus, they can see God all around them in every name and form. Those who can understand or "see" this truth with their intellect will release their mind's prior misunderstanding and create a new image that can now be seen more clearly with their "mind's eye." They can see God in everything. And if God is all and is in all, what does it matter if one person looks up into space, another looks at the earth, another looks at a statue, or another looks within? No matter where they look, they are all looking at the same thing. This "God" can be seen simultaneously from a pantheistic, polytheistic, monotheistic, and even an atheistic point of view without conflict or contradiction.

THE EMBODIED SOUL

In some ancient texts, the soul is a thing risked in battle and lost in death. In other texts, it is the thing that departs from a person at the time of death, where it either experiences happiness forever in a heaven far away, a pitiful existence in a hell far away or lingers around the Earth as a kind of shadowy cloud like a ghost, helping or hindering those nearby. But a commentary on another ancient text called the Kena Upanishad offers a more logical and, in my opinion, a more believable description of the embodied soul. In his translation, Swami Paramananda reveals, "Brahman (God) is the vast ocean of being, on which rise numberless ripples and waves of manifestation. From the smallest atomic form to a Deva or an Angel, all spring from that limitless ocean of Brahman, the inexhaustible source of life. No manifested form of life can be independent of its source, just as no wave, however mighty, can be independent of the ocean."

As I read the verse, I recalled the story of a wave shared by Sarvapriyananda during a lecture that he gave in New York. Once long ago, the wind swept slowly across the ocean creating a wave. As the wave grew in size and moved slowly across the ocean, it looked around and noticed it was not alone. There were many other waves also heading in a similar direction. The newly created wave saw that

17

some of the other waves were smaller than it was, and that made the wave very proud of itself. The wave saw that some of the other waves were larger than it was, and that made the wave feel inferior. The wave noticed that it liked some waves more than others. The wave called the waves that it liked friends. The wave called the waves that it didn't like enemies. The wave continued giving names and meaning to the other waves and became very comfortable with its surroundings until the wave saw the beach and realized it would soon crash upon the shore and die. The wave became very frightened and cried, "I am going to die!"

Then suddenly, a wise wave approached the frightened wave and asked it, "What do you know about water?" The frightened wave said, "Why should I care about water? Can't you see that we will crash upon the shore and die? The wise wave said, "You should care about water because the entire ocean is composed of water, and water can never die. Water is immortal. Water will exist forever." The frightened wave said, "That is very good for water, but what does that have to do with me?" The wise wave said, "It is important to know because there is water in small waves and in big waves. There is water in good waves, and there is water in bad waves. There is water in all waves and everything that exists around you. There is even water in you.

Just look at yourself. The top of you is water, the middle of you is water, and even the bottom of you is water. Look carefully at yourself and see that you are entirely composed of water." As the wave looked carefully at itself, it suddenly realized that it was entirely composed of water and had always been a part of the immortal ocean. The wave then lost all fear and left only the name and form of "wave" to crash upon the shore while focusing inward towards the ocean.

Your perceived existence is similar to the wave in the story. Like the wave in the ocean, you believe you were born into a physical name and form called "body," looking outward at the experiential world all around you, and have not yet fully realized that you are part of a great ocean known as God that exists within you and all around you.

Modern science agrees with this analogy. Some in the scientific community have postulated that all things are but a manifestation of one energy, which is the totality of everything that exists. And what do waves depend upon for their appearance? Time, space, and causation. Without these, the name and form "wave" cannot exist. When the wind energy causes the wave to become apparent, the wave, as if by magic, suddenly appears to exist within space over time. And yet, this time, space, and causation exist in and around the "wave" as a part of the wave, like shadows. And when the wave reduces back into the ocean, time, space, and causation also appear to disappear because they can only exist as long as the wave exists. So, there is the ocean, and with space, time, and causation, there is a wave. And when the wave reduces, so does the space, time, and causation back into the ocean.

As the wave subsides and returns to the ocean, the form appears to vanish, and yet the form was not a delusion. So long as the wave was there, you were bound to see the name and form of "wave" instead of the ocean. Similarly, the entire universe, from the suns and stars down to your physical form, are merely the various names and forms that the absolute ocean known as God manifests from itself. In that way, the perceived material universe, including your perceived physical form, is like the waves that appear as a part of the whole. You, all conscious beings, all of the manifest and unmanifest, all of the known and unknown, the totality of all, including the embodied souls, are in reality only God.

Imagine looking out over a field full of clover on a foggy morning, the leaves covered by the morning dew. As the fog lifts and the sun begins to peek through, you can see that every clover leaf has a single dew drop on top. As you look more closely, you can see that each drop of water contains a reflection of the sun within. You know that the sun above is the true reality, and the suns appearing in the dew drops merely reflect the one real sun. It is like this with the embodied soul. God is the one true reality, and your embodied soul is like the reflection of God within you. Your embodied soul can be intellectually seen as your awareness, expressed outwardly as your individual consciousness. Your embodied soul is the space from where your consciousness is manifested. It is the space from where your understanding happens in you. It is the space within you that is deeper than thinking. In this regard, your embodied soul is an appearance of God that is primary to and independent of all the names and forms in the perceived universe.

Your embodied soul will not die when your physical body is considered dead. Like the water in the ocean, the embodied soul is eternal and everlasting. It is inconceivable; it temporarily interacts with this illusory world and cannot be affected by it. Your embodied soul is immortal and indestructible, and it dwells within the perceived body of everyone. For one who is born, physical death is unavoidable, but that cannot affect the embodied soul.

When human beings are said to be born, an aspect of God called the embodied soul appears to become embodied within the physical form by forming delicate connections with the intellect, the mind, the neurons of the brain, and the rest of the perceived physical body, in an infinitely more subtle way than the way smoke can dwell between sand in an hourglass. This delicate connection of awareness to the perceived physical world appears as consciousness. This consciousness then provides the embodied soul, awareness itself, the opportunity to experience and participate within a transactional medium, a transactional world. In this way, consciousness can appear to be the temporary interplay between the embodied soul and the perceived physical world.

Imagine a Doctor of Anesthesiology placing a patient under anesthesia for a condition requiring surgery. The chemical administered to the patient by the anesthesiologist disrupts the delicate connection between the patient's apparent consciousness and its connections to the perceived physical world. Under anesthesia, the patient is said to have lost consciousness. It is as if the patient has gone into a state of deep sleep. Whether the patient is unconscious for one minute or twelve hours, when the patient awakens, the patient always states that it seems no time has passed. The patient will have remembered experiencing absolutely nothing and will say that it felt like they left and came back in the blink of an eye. This occurs because the soul without the body is like the ocean without the wave; causation, space, and time no longer exist. To the patient, the space of the perceived physical world and time did not exist because their soul did not participate in it. The patient's perceived state of deep sleep was not the absence of experience. It was the experience of absence.

The perceived physical world and all in it, including your physical form, is only an appearance, like the wave, and the viewer that experiences the perceived physical world is you, the awareness. Under anesthesia, the patient's embodied soul merely lost its delicate connections for a time, and those connections returned after the drug lost its effectiveness. The proof of the existence of the embodied soul is not discovered when the patient loses consciousness. The evidence of the existence of the embodied soul is discovered when the patient's consciousness returns without guidance or assistance.

In much the same manner, if there is sufficient disruption of the perceived physical body in any event that leads to perceived physical death, the embodied soul simply loses its apparent connection to the perceived physical world in the same way. When the embodied soul is liberated from the body at the time of bodily death, nothing can accompany it, not memories of good times, bad times, mistakes, or any of your other memories. Those remain with the neurons of the perceived physical body. You will recall nothing and become one with the ocean again.

Some mistakenly believe the perceived physical body creates the consciousness manifested from the embodied soul. That logic is as foolish as watching 100 people walk through a door, one at a time, and concluding as each person passed through the door that they were all created by the door simply because you could not see where they came from before they reached the door. Some hold on to this misunderstanding because even though they cannot see where the people came from, they can become preoccupied with studying the door.

To better illustrate the point, imagine if the entire population of humans on Earth today was each given a cellular phone and somebody told all 7.7 billion people to call each other simultaneously. This event would be similar to the neurons of an individual's brain communicating simultaneously due to some external input received by the senses. Would all those phones working together simultaneously create a new kind of consciousness? Of course not. In the same way, it seems absurd to think that the communication of the brain's neurons creates the consciousness within sentient beings.

Imagine that you purchased a lamp. Most easily understand that someone cannot turn a lamp on without the lamp being plugged into an electrical outlet first because the lamp is only a machine and cannot become operational or give off light without electricity. All your household appliances rely upon electricity from a power plant far away before they can be turned on and operational. But once you plug the lamp into the power source and flip the switch on, the lamp becomes a working machine and converts the electrical energy into light as if by magic. Notice that if you unplug the lamp, the lamp stops working, but all of the other appliances in the house that are still plugged in and turned on continue working. This reveals that even though the lamp is no longer operational, the electricity continues to flow throughout the house, just to other appliances. A similar kind of thing occurs in perceived physical death. In perceived physical death, some part or parts of the machine, the individual human frame, no longer function or have been damaged to the point where the entire physical body can no longer act as a medium for the embodied soul. It does not mean the soul dies. Like electricity, the soul continues to flow from its source regardless of the state of the body.

We have all heard about instances in the hospital when some human beings were considered dead by the doctor when their heart stopped, but then, for some unexplainable reason, they regained consciousness. This occurred because the embodied soul was freed from the physical body at the time of death in the same manner as when one goes under anesthesia, and some, when the physical body's function is restored to sufficient working levels, regain their delicate connections and appear to reawaken once again.

While you may believe that the perceived physical world can affect your body, it cannot affect your embodied soul. The embodied soul does not die when the physical body is considered dead. Like the water in the ocean, the embodied soul is eternal and everlasting. Your embodied soul is inconceivable; it temporarily interacts with this illusory world and cannot be affected by it. The embodied soul is immortal and indestructible. It is an aspect of the great ocean known as God, and it dwells within everyone's perceived body. For one who is born, physical death is inevitable, but that cannot affect the embodied soul.

THE HOLY TRINITY

Once, many years ago, there was a child who was given a dog for his birthday. His father gave him the dog and said owning a dog would teach the boy responsibility and provide a best friend to hunt and play with. The father said dogs were the best pets in the world because they would be loyal, kind, and better than cats. He said if you broke your leg in the woods, a dog would either run and get help or lay next to you so that you wouldn't freeze overnight while waiting for help to arrive. He said if you broke your leg in the woods and had a cat, the cat would ignore you until you died of exposure and eat you. Needless to say, the boy never desired a cat.

But then, after many years, the child had grown into an older man. As an old man at sixty-two years of age, he retired and bought a little ranch. The ranch's backyard was eight acres across and surrounded by thousands of thick trees that abutted a wildlife preserve. In this private sanctuary, the old man could see mountain lions pass through the backyard from his back porch as they roamed away from the mountains. Just in the wild cat species alone, the old man also spotted bobcats and ocelots that looked like a wild version of a grey-brown tabby cat passing less than 100 feet from the back porch. While on the property one day, the old man's grandson discovered what appeared to be a wild baby ocelot hiding underneath the tractor. Excitedly, they caught it as a family, only to discover it was an abandoned ordinary tabby cat.

The old man's wife and grandchildren loved the cat, and soon, after the proper shots and evaluation by the veterinarian, the cat was named "Ringtail." As Ringtail grew, so did his range of exploration. By the time Ringtail was an adult, he had spent some of his nights traveling' from one neighbor's ranch to another to share and receive a little affection with the neighbor's cats. Late one afternoon, as the old man was driving down his long country road toward the highway, he saw Ringtail three ranches down in the neighbor's backyard, relaxing with their cat on the neighbor's lap. It was at that moment that the old man had the epiphany. When he was a little boy, his grandmother told him his grandfather was catting around town; that was exactly what she meant. If the old man had been convinced as a child never to own a cat, the man would likely never would have understood the meaning of 'catting around.' All of those who have never owned a cat are likely in the same predicament. This story is meant to reveal how easily the meanings of sayings can get lost in one generation, let alone over two thousand years.

For example, many non-Christians, and many Christians for that matter, struggle with the ancient meaning of the Holy Trinity. The word "Trinity" in the Catholic term "Holy Trinity" comes from the Latin noun, "Trinitas" meaning "three are one." Jim Akin, a writer for the catholic news agency CNA, gave the Catholic Church's interpretation in the national catholic register. On May 26, 2024, he wrote, "The Church expresses her trinitarian faith by professing a belief in the oneness of God in whom there are three Persons: Father,

Son, and Holy Spirit. The three divine Persons are only one God because each of them equally possesses the fullness of the one and indivisible divine nature. They are really distinct from each other by reason of the relations which place them in correspondence to each other. The Father generates the Son; the Son is generated by the Father; the Holy Spirit proceeds from the Father and the Son" (No. 48)."

Perplexing descriptions like this may be the source of the confusion. So, to more accurately interpret the meaning of the Holy Trinity and clear up any misunderstanding that may have occurred over time, I will reframe the intellectual point of view so that there may be a beneficial paradigm shift in the approach to the subject. This new point of view will be necessary to unpack a logical line of reasoning that will provide a more precise and understandable portrait of the actual meaning.

Step 1: let us begin by imagining you are looking at a mirror. As you look at the mirror, three things should become apparent. There is you, the reality. There is the mirror that acts as a reflective surface. And there is an image of you that appears in the mirror, created by light, that is reflected back to you from the mirror. Step 2: let us now imagine how a single thought in your mind can be similar to looking at a mirror. There is your awareness, the reality; there is your mind that acts as a reflective surface of sorts; and there is light created by your desire that shines upon the mind, appearing as an image, as it is reflected back to the awareness from the mind. The one notable difference between looking outwardly at a mirror and looking inside at one's thoughts is that thoughts appear to have three seemingly separate components, while in reality, they are only one because they are all found only within you. Step 3: In the same way you realized in step two that a single thought within you can have three seemingly separate components, an apparent universe can exist within the one God while appearing as three separate components, only on an infinitely larger scale. God appears as the omnipresent sentient awareness (microcosm), the matter and energy of the body/mind, and the matter and energy of the external universe (macrocosm), while in reality being only The One.

God has become all, and it is God that is all. God is the instrumental cause of the perceived universe and the material cause. In his 1895 lecture in New York, Vivekananda stated, "That which you believe you experience all around you is simply the effect appearing different from the cause. Since the effect is never different from the cause and the cause is never different from the effect, the effect can be nothing more than the cause appearing in another form." For example, if the cause is sand, sand can be heated and eventually formed into glass. Glass, in this case, is the effect of heated sand. When the glass is repeatedly smashed with a stone, it can eventually be broken back down into its causal state of sand and heat. In this way, glass is the appearance of sand in another form.

Let us look at the ancient Hebrew Torah for more insight. The JPS translation states in the opening chapter of the book of Genesis, "1:1 When God began to create heaven and earth 2 the earth being unformed and void, with darkness over the surface of the deep and a wind from God sweeping over the water 3 God said, "Let there be light"; and there was light." The first thing one could misunderstand as it relates to this opening statement is that the surface of the deep does not describe whether or not we are talking about a deep within

God or a deep outside of God. That could lead some to believe that the surface of the deep is something other than God, wrongly creating a kind of duality, God, and something else. But, Since God is all, there can be no internal or external as it relates to God. So, everything must be within God. Second, the earth being unformed and void does not mean it is nonexistent. It merely means it is not yet formed, much like a subatomic quantum field, until gross matter appears to be manifested from it. Third, the wind from God sweeping over the water can also mean the same thing that happens when a human being is trying to recall something in their head. When human beings are trying to remember something, anything, they look within themselves and sweep over the face of the waters within their mind, looking for a solution.

To better understand this, let us bring the idea down to scale. Instead of imagining yourself in the middle of darkness hovering over the face of the deep, imagine yourself in an isolation tank. In an isolation tank, there is nothing to see, hear, touch, taste, or smell. You are in darkness and experiencing nothing from the senses. But in this apparent darkness and nothingness, there is still something. There is you, and that means within you, there can be light, the light of your imagination. If you desire to see anything, merely say the word, and you will project the appearance of an image brightly onto the mind. It is common knowledge that the mind produces the appearance of a related image for every word. Say cat, and the desire from deep within your awareness will project the appearance of a cat onto the mind that will be reflected back to you, the awareness, by the mind. The appearance of the cat is not the reality. The appearance is instead merely a reflection of the desire projected from within the awareness.

This scenario is very similar to that within God, just on a grander scale. In the same way that a human being can project the appearance of a universe within themselves, God can project the appearance of an infinite universe within God. This would also help to explain the legendary speed with which God created the infinite universe.

The Christian New Testament contains a similar translation of Genesis 1:4: "And God said, 'Let there be light,' and there was light." This translation reveals that the word of God is the cause, and the image within God is the effect. In a similar way that saying any word will cause a corresponding image to appear inside your mind, God's word caused the infinite universe to appear within God. God's word is the cause, and the reflected image is the effect. All reflections called matter and energy are not independent things in and of themselves. They are simply reflections called nature when seen as the effect. In this way, God becomes both the subject and the object.

At this point, it might be natural to ask, "If God is the only one, how can there be so many?" To answer this, imagine looking again over an enormous meadow covered with millions of clovers on a foggy morning. In the morning, as the fog rises and the sun breaks through, there are billions of drops of water on every leaf of the clovers. On closer examination, you can see a reflection of the sun in every drop of water. You know that there is only one sun, and the suns that appear to be in the individual drops of water are only a reflection of the actual sun. It is similar to the infinite perceived external universe, humanity, and God. The perceived external universe can be seen as the meadow and the clovers, the drops of water can be seen as the physical forms of all sentient beings, and the reflection of the sun within the drops can be seen as the awareness of God within all sentient beings, reflected as their consciousness.

Since everything is of God, from God, and in God, God is the one true reality of the perceived matter and energy of the macrocosm, the perceived matter and energy in the body/mind, and the perceived awareness within the microcosm. These three appear to be different from one another, while in reality, they are the One. This Knowledge enabled Jesus to say, "I and God are one." Jesus understood that the reflected awareness within him was the same as the actual awareness of God. Imagine looking at a mirror again. As you look at the mirror, you see a reflection of yourself. You believe that you are the reality and the image you see in the mirror is only a reflection of that reality. You know that you can exist without the reflection in the mirror, but the reflection in the mirror cannot exist without you. So, the fact that the reflection exists in the mirror infers that you are standing in front of the mirror. The reflection is only because of you.

Similarly, if the awareness within Jesus exists, it is only because of the infinite awareness of God. God's infinite awareness is the one actual reality, and Jesus' awareness is the reflection of that reality. Jesus and God both exist as the one. But isn't it wrong to insinuate that the reflection is the reality? How can Jesus say he and God are one when Jesus is only the reflection? Easily, because the reflection knows that the awareness of God is with him, or he wouldn't exist as a conscious being. Pure awareness is undoubtedly separate from reflected awareness, but reflected awareness is never separate from pure awareness.

In the past, during the time of Jesus, when Christians said there is a Holy Trinity composed of the Father, the Son, and the Holy Spirit, it was more likely than not meant in the common-sense light I presented. However, over time, the original meaning must have been lost, and most humans began imagining it as three separate beings. But now, we can interpret the Father as the macrocosm, the Son as the body/mind, and the Holy Spirit as the awareness within the microcosm, all appearances of one actual reality, God. In this way, these three seemingly separate names in the Holy Trinity are not three separate beings; they are merely a misunderstood analogy that Jesus Christ intended to describe that which appears as three, being, in reality, only the one gazing upon itself.

THE AFTERLIFE

There is likely no greater fear known to humanity than the fear of death. For everyone who is born, death is an inevitable reality. This fear of dying is a significant problem. The historical solution for most of humanity has been to conclude that an individual identity or soul exists within every human being, separate from all other identities or souls that continue to exist after the death of the physical body. For some, this solution seems to have nicely reduced the fear of death to tolerable levels. Sadly, this solution to the problem of death may have created as much fear and maybe even more anxiety in some human beings than the idea of death itself.

One of the reasons for this newfound fear and anxiety is that each religion has wildly different descriptions of the afterlife. The afterlife that religious followers are told they will be subjected to depends upon many factors, such as the religion the human being chose to be affiliated with before death and the morphologic characteristics of the soul in question. For example, some Eastern religions believe that there are seven individual types of souls, and you can only be one soul type. The amount of the soul that survives differs between religions as well. It can be an element, a soul, or a spirit. If that isn't enough to cause concern, the location where each religion claims its followers' spirit goes also varies between the different religions. The Abrahamic religions, like the Hebrews, Catholics, Christians, and Muslims, believe that this individual spirit goes to a location built by their version of God, far removed from the world we all experience. To them, there is one location where some individual spirits are well rewarded for eternity for their actions and beliefs during their brief life called heaven and another location where some individual souls are punished for eternity for their actions and beliefs during their brief life called hell. Salvation from going to hell after violating the religious rules can only be achieved by voluntary open apologies, specific rituals, or penances approved by the very religion that created hell in the first place. Religions from the East, like Hinduism, Buddhism, Jainism, and Sikhism, believe that each soul comes back to the world as the same individual, but in a different form and with varying amounts of pleasure or suffering owed to them; not dependent upon a God, but dependent upon the individuals' actions and beliefs in their prior lives. If you are outstanding, you return to a prosperous and healthy life. If you are naughty, you come back in poverty, disfigured, with some genetic illness, or as something less than human, like an animal or insect. Followers of these Eastern Religions generally believe that their soul is trapped in this continuous cycle of life and death until it can earn its way to their version of liberation through activities approved by their religion. The one thing that the various religions generally agree about is that each soul carries the human being's identity around after death, like a kind of identification card, wherever it goes.

If, at first glance, you think these solutions might seem a bit far-fetched or incredibly ridiculous, you had better keep that to yourself. Horrific wars and terrible atrocities have been waged upon non-believers throughout history in the name of each religion's defense of their specific religious dogma. But is it really necessary to invent a separate thing, a separate individual soul, to assuage the fear of death? Not at all.

Let's look at the same concept in a different way. What if your soul is not a separate and individual kind of thing? What if the thing that has historically been called a soul is merely a part of something much greater that never has to experience death in the first place? What if the thing that everyone has been looking at as an individual wave is only an outward appearance of a great ocean? For example, when waves take form in the ocean, they are often considered to be something other than the ocean, something in addition to the ocean. Something separate from the ocean. They are even given their own name, "Wave". And while an infinite number of waves will come into and out of existence, every single one of them has always been and always will be, in reality, only the ocean. The name and form of a wave is merely the outward appearance, a different aspect of the ocean. This different aspect of the ocean creates the appearance of an independent thing. When a wave is considered to be born, a different aspect of the ocean appears, but the ocean itself remains the ocean. Nothing has been gained or lost. The ocean goes nowhere when the wave crashes on the beach and is considered dead. The death of the wave, like the birth of the wave, was only an outward appearance of the ocean.

Similarly to the wave, your outward appearance, or your name and physical form, is from God, of God, and in God, and so is your embodied soul. God is the great unchanging ocean of sorts, and you are an appearance of that. So, when your perceived physical form is considered to be born into the perceived physical world, your physical form, like the wave, is only an appearance of a different aspect of the great unchanging ocean known as God. When your physical form is considered to have died in the perceived physical world, only the appearance of the infinite ocean, seen as your physical body, appears to die. The reality of you, the awareness that religions call the soul within, can never die because it has always been and always will be, in reality, a part of the great ocean known as God.

Instead of discussing the subject in the abstract, let's look at it from a commonly shared experience everyone can likely relate to. Try to recall your best night's sleep. You slept like a log. You dozed off, and in what seemed like an instant, you opened your eyes, and the entire perceived physical world moved forward eight hours or so without you going anywhere or experiencing any of it. It was as if the last eight hours didn't exist at all. This is because the perceived physical world's time and space didn't exist to your awareness. Your perceived physical body was lying peacefully in bed. Your embodied soul went nowhere and spent the night peacefully unattached to the perceived physical world. It is the same in perceived physical death. In a similar way that you go to sleep and become peacefully unattached to the perceived physical world while asleep, in perceived physical death, your embodied soul also becomes peacefully unattached to the perceived physical world. You go nowhere, and your embodied soul remains completely unaffected. This is not the absence of experience but simply the experience of absence. In perceived physical death, you will close your eyes as your perceived physical body appears to die to others, and you will be considered ocean again. But don't worry; this ocean of awareness known as GOD continually has new aspects of itself, new names and forms called waves that come and go, while all the time remaining the unchanging ocean.

The most important part to remember is that your perceived physical form is part of the material energy of God, and your awareness is also an aspect of the great ocean known as God. Similarly, a wave can be seen as an appearance of the ocean on the surface of the ocean while remaining the ocean, you and God can be seen as different manifestations of the same thing. You were wrongly taught that you have a soul that is separate from God and others, that comes and goes from an illusory world, when, in reality, you are a part of God and go nowhere. The awareness within you has always been a part of the eternal, indestructible, immeasurable, and everlasting ocean known as God. From this new perspective, you can now understand that life and death are only an appearance; the time between the two can be heaven on earth, there is no afterlife to worry about, and you can live life fearlessly forever if you choose.

HEAVEN IS ALL AROUND

There is no afterlife. There is only God and the perception of an experiential world. This means that all the speculation about heaven and hell by science and religion was merely speculation. All the stories about heaven and hell were simply fantastic tales told by those who likely wanted to believe in something better than the world they believed they were experiencing. Whenever the various Abrahamic religions spoke of far-off locations where punishment and reward were doled out to the masses after death in accordance with the rules imposed by some celestial judge, they were entirely wrong. That is likely one reason why, over the ages, when reasonable people took the time to stop and think about religious claims regarding heaven and hell, they were usually left with what can be described, at best, as uncertainty and at worst with the kind of mistrust that led to a good percentage of those religious seekers turning their backs on their religion altogether.

It might seem that when religions made these claims, they were intentionally dishonest or manipulative, but that is untrue. They were simply a little lost. To better understand the point, imagine an ordinary English-speaking tourist couple trying to drive a car in a foreign Spanish country. They are on vacation in a small town they have never visited before. The GPS is not working; the map is in Spanish, and they do not speak or read Spanish well, so they naturally become a bit lost. When they finally pull over to ask for directions from one of the locals, the local reads the map and clearly says, "Derecho," which means straight ahead. However, with his limited Spanish, the driver understands the word Derecho (straight ahead) to mean Derecha (turn to the right). So, instead of going straight ahead as instructed, the driver mistakenly turns to the right at the nearest intersection. At the next intersection, he turns right, and at the next intersection, he does the same; he turns right. Lo and behold, he ends up in front of the person who gave him the directions earlier. Because the driver misunderstood one letter of one word, the tourists ended up going in circles. It is like this with religions. Because they misunderstood the meaning of some aspect of their bibles or texts, they innocently took a wrong turn and have been going around in circles ever since.

Given this knowledge, one has to ask oneself, is there a heaven at all? Is there a hell at all? Does the realization that there is no afterlife per se mean that the ideas of heaven and hell are moot? Who can we turn to for better directions? To this question, there is good news. A well-known historical figure named Jesus solved this problem in the book, "The Gospel of Thomas." In the 3rd of 114 sayings recorded in this ancient text, Jesus said, "If those who lead you say unto you: Behold, the Kingdom is in heaven, then the birds of the heaven will be before you. If they say unto you: It is in the sea, the fish will be before you. But the Kingdom is within you, and it is outside of you. When you know yourselves, then shall you be known, and you shall know that you are the sons of the living Father. But if ye do not know yourselves, then you are in poverty, and you are poverty." I will unpack the logic behind this statement so that you may understand precisely why it can be considered good news.

Let us begin by reframing the intellectual point of view and define heaven not as an abstract possibility that exists within the unknowable but as the reality that already exists around us that everyone can know or has known. This knowable definition of heaven is, "The contentment and lasting peace experienced in life that results from returning mentally to reflect upon the origins of a desire and the beauty of its completion." Now that the proper definition is in place, we can begin unpacking.

All of your deepest desires begin within your awareness. They come from that place within you that is deeper than thinking. As each desire moves outward, the desire moves from thought to decision to action. Your actions then begin to affect and change the perceived physical world around you until your desire becomes manifest. You are continually rearranging the perceived physical world by your desires. However, the object of your deepest desire will become what you desire at that specific moment and not what you may desire at a different moment. This can easily create unhappiness rather than peace.

For example, when a girl was young, she desired to be a nurse. Over time, she became a great nurse, but her career did not bring her contentment or lasting peace. She became unhappy because she could see from this new perspective that being a nurse was nothing like what she thought it would be as a child. Now a young woman, she believed she could find contentment and lasting peace by achieving more than just being a nurse. So, she desired to be a nurse practitioner and became a great nurse practitioner over time. Yet this career did not bring her contentment or lasting peace either. She was unhappy because she realized, from this new perspective, that being a nurse practitioner was nothing like what she thought it would be as a young woman. Now an older woman, she believed she could find contentment and lasting peace by achieving more than she dreamed of as a young woman. So, she desired to be in the position of a medical doctor, and so on. Like the woman in this story, this is the progressive unhappiness that most humans experience when they look at their blessings from the wrong perspective.

They are unhappy because they fail to realize that the perceived physical world has provided them with an interactional space that allows them to manifest all of their desires. They are unhappy, even though the perceived physical world allowed all of their desires to manifest and will continue to allow them to manifest as long as there is no conflict within them that would prevent their desires from coming into being. They cannot appreciate receiving everything they have ever truly wanted.

This is because it takes time to manifest desires, years in fact, and by the time their desires become manifest, instead of being content, they are looking forward to new desires and have long forgotten the reasons for their earlier desires. Their unhappiness results from receiving the object of their desires long after the reason for their desires has faded from their memories. They are unable to stay in one mental place long enough to marvel at the perceived physical world around them, which continually allows their desires to manifest in due time. They should stand in amazement and be overcome with joy at this never-ending miracle. They should be able to see that they are living in heaven, yet they believe they are living in hell.

They wrongly believe they are living in hell because they have forgotten why they had their desire in the first place. They are looking at what they desired from a new position that they put themselves in and cannot recall the original context of their prior desire. The nurse could not recall from the context of the young girl how truly wonderful it would be to become a nurse. She could not remember her desire from the context that she desired it as a young girl. If she could think back in time and take herself to her mindset as a young girl when she was dreaming about becoming a nurse, she would see that she was in heaven every day she was able to be a nurse.

Most can recall having a dream of becoming something or getting something they wanted more than anything else. But not many can remember the joy and contentment they felt in the moment that they actually received it. Getting a new job, a big promotion, a big bonus, a new degree, certification, or award was heavenly. But once the moment was over and done, the realities surrounding their desire soon became apparent, and they began to think about how ignorant they were of the realities that surrounded their desire. After that big promotion, the challenges of the job became way more stressful; the hours became longer, and the load much heavier. Instead of enjoying the gift of the new job, most soon become unhappy and begin to convince themselves that they would be much happier if they only had something else. They forgot how much they dreamed about the big promotion, extra money, respect, and security of a better retirement. They are living in heaven because all of their desires have become manifest, and yet they are frustrated and unhappy because they cannot see it while looking at it from the wrong perspective and in the wrong context. Heaven is all around them, yet they remain blind to its existence.

If you wish to experience heaven on earth, you only need to return mentally to the moment that any desire arose within you and recall the original context of the desire. Then, connect that moment with the moment that your desire became manifest in the perceived physical world, and you will quickly realize that Jesus was right. Heaven has been all around you and even within you this entire time. You will not only experience heaven; you will also experience completion.

REINCARNATION

There is no reincarnation, at least not in the way different religions have historically described it. This is because your individual life is, in reality, only an appearance of self that emerges over time and represents nothing more than your ego as it is presented to you, the awareness, by the mind.

Ego can be defined simply as how a person perceives him or herself. It is the product of the education administered to you by others that is then presented to your awareness by your mind. Your ego can be considered yours, but the ego is not you, the awareness. Any time anyone allows others to define them, they are staring directly at the source of what can be considered their ego. All of the good and bad things people have said about them, all of the nicknames they've been given, and everything everyone around them said they could or couldn't do, when accepted by them, became a reflection of themselves. Not because of the truth or validity of what was said but because of their acceptance.

When anyone shares their time, thoughts, and feelings with others, the responses of those others act as a reflection of themselves that they choose to accept and begin to believe is them. This is their ego. From the beginning of each perceived life up until perceived death, the education that trusted loved ones like Parents, relatives, friends, and co-workers confer upon a person directly affects the way humans see themselves, the confidence they have in themselves, their belief systems, and the love of self or their lack thereof. Their belief in their attributes are easily manipulated because they freely allow others to define them. In that way, ego is nothing more than an illusory reflection of what one considers the self, as reflected through the teaching of others. But ego is not you, the awareness.

You, the awareness, can never be seen directly by you, in a similar way that your eyes can never be seen directly by you. You cannot see your eyes directly, but you can always see because of them, so you know they are there. While you can never see your eyes directly, you can see your eyes as a reflected image, like the reflection in a mirror or the reflection seen in a calm pool of water. To see a reflection of you, the awareness, imagine waves taking form in the ocean. As the waves appear to come into existence, they are often considered to be something other than the ocean, something in addition to the ocean. They are even given their own name: wave. While an infinite number of waves will come into and out of existence throughout time, every single one of them always has been and always will be, in reality, only the ocean. The name and form of a wave are merely a different appearance of the ocean. This different appearance of the ocean creates the appearance of an independent thing. When a wave is considered to be created, a distinct expression of the ocean seems to appear, but the ocean itself remains the one true reality. Nothing has been gained or lost. When the wave crashes on the beach, the wave appears to go out of existence, but the reality is that the ocean went nowhere. The ocean remains the ocean, and nothing has been gained or lost. The death of the wave, like the birth of the wave, was only an appearance within the ocean.

Similarly, your perceived physical form and even the whole of creation are from God, of God, and in God. God is the great unchanging ocean of sorts. So, when a human being is considered to be born into the perceived physical world, it is only the appearance of a different aspect of God. When the human being is considered to be dead in the future, the ego, the name, and form will cease to exist, but God alone will remain. Despite this reality, the ego creates the illusion of something other than God.

Some Hindus wrongly believe the proof of reincarnation is revealed in animal instincts. They say because a turtle, at birth, knows how to break out of its shell, crawl out of the sand, and work its way to the ocean alone without assistance, it proves that the new-born turtle was born with some prior knowledge. They say it is the same with the chicken that can pick up food once it hatches. Their argument is as follows: for the baby turtle to know how to get across the beach into the ocean and the chick to know how to eat, they must have brought the information with them from another prior life. This argument is false on a lower level because it assumes that this knowledge applies across all forms of life, and it is untrue on a higher level because it wrongly assumes the chick and turtle are something other than appearances within God.

First, the examples of the turtle and chick having prior knowledge are false because they contradict another false belief in Hinduism, their belief that their future level of reincarnation has something to do with the karma they produced in a prior life. For example, Hindus generally believe that a human being will be punished in the next life for the bad deeds of the current life by reincarnating as something less than human. If you are bad, you might come back as a goat. If you are very naughty, you might come back as a worm. However, if you are good, you might come back with more wealth and comfort. If you are outstanding in this life, you might return as a God (small g). So, what good would the knowledge one attained as a naughty human being who lived his entire life on a snow-covered mountain do if he were to suddenly return as a turtle in a shell, one foot under sand near a beach? The prior knowledge the human being possessed would be useless.

Second, the concept of reincarnation wrongly implies that there is something other than God. The Ancient Hindu books called the Vedas give fascinating insight into what most Hindus have missed. The ancient books reveal that the entire known and unknown universe is composed of three basic components. Akasha, Prana and Purusha.

Akasha, according to the Vedas, is considered to be the omnipresent. Everything that has form and is the result of combination evolved from Akasha. Akasha becomes the gases that become the liquids, that become the solids. Akasha becomes the oceans, mountains, deserts, sun, stars, and even the bodies of animals, plants, and humans. Every object with or without name and form in the known universe evolves from Akasha. Akasha is so ultra-fine that it is beyond perception. This ancient information matches quite nicely with today's modern scientific theories on the subatomic quantum field.

Prana is the infinite, omnipresent, manifesting power of the universe. According to the Vedas, at the beginning and end of each cycle of the perceived infinite universe, everything becomes Akasha again, and all the forces in the universe resolve back into the Prana. From Prana, everything that we call energy evolves, everything that we call force. The Prana manifests as motion, gravity, magnetism, electricity, nuclear fission, nerve conduction, and even thought. Prana is the totality of all of the forces in the universe once they have returned to their original state.

The third and likely most important of the three is Purusha. It is important because Purusha does not exist. Purusha is existence itself. The whole of the infinite universe begins with awareness and goes all the way up to gross matter. The part of you known as the embodied soul is Purusha. Purusha appears as all matter (Akasha) and force (Prana). Akasha and Prana exist because of Purusha. The Purusha alone is self-luminous and gives its light to everything. Existence and knowledge are not the qualities of Purusha but its essence. Christians know this Purusha as God, and the Hebrews know this Purusha as Yahweh (the self-existent one). The Torah, the ancient text in Christianity and Judaism, states, "In the beginning, God created the heavens and the earth." This agrees with the ancient Hindu Vedas. If "In the beginning" is time, "God" is the self-existent one or Purusha, "Created" is the infinite, omnipresent manifesting power that evolves action called Prana, and "The Heavens and the earth" are the objective result of the combination of Akasha, then the ancient texts all validate one another.

Essentially, all matter throughout the perceived universe, is the result of one fundamental matter called Akasha; all force is the outcome of one fundamental force called Prana, and that which is beyond Akasha and Prana is Purusha. Purusha does not create Akasha and Prana; Akasha and Prana are merely an appearance of Purusha. This reveals that time, space, matter, energy, force, all that exists, and all that is yet to manifest exist only within Purusha (God) as a different appearance or manifestation of God. Since everything is from God, of God, and in God, what can reincarnate? Like waves that are, in reality, only ocean; everything in existence is only an appearance of God. So, when someone argues that the turtle or the chicken had prior knowledge, the Christians, the Hebrews, and the Hindus should now understand that it is only God who has actual knowledge and existence. Thus, the idea of reincarnation of beings other than God based upon the Hindu assertion of prior knowledge is false.

Try to recall one of the dreams you experienced while sleeping. In your dream state, you created a world that existed only within your mind. You saw people, places, and things throughout the dream that seemed incredibly real but were, in reality, merely a product of your creation. Some of the characters you encountered in your dream were frightening, some were loving, some were hateful, and some made you sad. But upon waking, you quickly recognized that the dream was not real. You realize that the characters in your dream were an exclusive product of your mind, created by you, then presented to your awareness while sleeping. It is easily understood that the characters in your dream will not end up somewhere else, at some later date in time, in someone else's dream. The characters in your dream will not be punished or rewarded later in someone else's dream for what they did or didn't do in your dream.

It is similar in the perceived physical world. As trillions and trillions of what seem to be separate conscious beings continually appear to be born and then die in the illusory world, they are not reborn in some other place on the planet at some unknown future date again, waiting to be punished or rewarded for their previous life. That is only an illusion presented to awareness by the ego. Instead, much like the dream state you are very familiar with, an infinite variety of expressions of God, seen as conscious beings, appear to come into and out of a perceived existence within God because there is only an appearance of life and death within the perceived physical world for the one ocean known as God to experience.

Those who hold on to the idea of individual reincarnation are simply victims of the fear created when they cling to the false notion of self as a real thing rather than the truth of their divine nature. Holding tightly to their perceived individual identity, their ego, they attempt to reduce their fears by protecting their identity and creating a multitude of false concepts that help them overcome their fear. Essentially, their version of reincarnation is a kind of fiction that provides them a way to manage the fear of death created by their ignorance and doubts.

KARMA

Karma can be defined in many different ways. To some, it is seen as good things that happen to good people and bad things that happen to bad people. Others apply it in the same manner that heaven and hell are applied in some religions. For example, when one person comes across another person suffering from the cold because they have no jacket, the one viewing the suffering person will often use their respective religion to help distance themselves from showing compassion or getting involved. They will say, "It is the other person's Karma." They misuse the idea of karma to convince themselves that the other person must be suffering from or because of something they did in the past or in a past life. Therefore, there is no way their assistance or compassion could change the situation. Those human beings use karma to rationalize their doubts and their subsequent refusal to be responsible or act with compassion.

Karma can also be seen as the law of cause and effect, creating a structure within the perceived physical world. In this way, karma provides a feedback mechanism in the perceived physical world that allows humans to live within the interactional medium and experience it as they choose. Karma allows one the opportunity to take actions, experience success, and enjoy the fruits of one's actions or identify mistakes, put out new energy, and new actions to diminish, reverse, or wipe away the waves of bad karma created with prior actions.

It is common knowledge that a child should attend school and get at least a basic education. It is well known that education is for the long-term benefit of the child and society. It is also well known that it is not the location or type of school provided to the child that ultimately determines the child's grades. How the child behaves at school over time, regardless of the obstacles to learning, determines their grades. If the child applies themselves faithfully to the challenges at school, the child will get high marks and experience peace. If the child fails to make an effort, regardless of the reason, their grades will suffer until they change their academic behavior. In this case, Karma would be the scores the child earned and the feedback with each new season or semester, giving the child a new opportunity to improve their grades.

Examples of this kind of karma can also be found in the health of the human body. If you carefully care for your body through your actions, your body will achieve and maintain optimal health and be at peace. However, if you smoke tobacco, for example, each cigarette you ingest will act in a small way to damage your body until the cumulative effect is disease and suffering. Imagine two armies facing one another. One army would be the body's lung cells, and the other would be cigarettes. It takes thousands of cigarettes to kill thousands of lung cells, but if you are determined to smoke the cigarettes, then you have sided with the cigarette army, and the lungs are doomed to suffer. Likewise, if you side with the lungs and exercise the determination to avoid smoking, then you have sided with the lungs, and your body will be at peace.

Wars like those that happen to human beings' physical frames in the perceived physical world do not only happen in days or weeks. These wars can occur at the same relative speed at which trees grow, taking months or even years. Therefore, the results of these wars are often not seen for weeks or years, and recovery usually takes around the same time to reverse the effects when possible. This type of karma can be easily seen in many physical ailments, and it is so obvious that children are taught these lessons in their health classes. With the knowledge the children gain, they may use their intellects to avoid improper action throughout their lives, preventing some illnesses and the resultant suffering from having any chance of occurring at all.

Similarly, karma can be seen in all other actions occurring while awake in the perceived physical world. Treating loved ones poorly over time will lead to loneliness. Failing to perform your best at your tasks will lead to unhappiness, and mistreating your neighbors may lead to incarceration. Conversely, giving love and compassion will lead to receiving love and compassion. Sharing will lead to wealth, and offering forgiveness will lead to receiving forgiveness.

Some have mistakenly equated life's challenges and life's difficulties with bad karma. They believe that those who do good deeds must get good, and those who do bad deeds must get bad. They cannot understand why someone good must experience bad and why someone bad gets to experience good. This is due to their mistaken logic. The wise understand that those who do good deeds must also do so in the face of what they consider bad or difficult. They choose to have faith that the entire illusory world is an experience that they do not fully understand. They look at their challenges and difficulties with faith that their thoughts of bad karma could only be due to doubts created by an error on their part because of their lack of understanding.

Paradoxical views of the perceived physical world are often played out in life as bad karma because many humans simultaneously hold on to multiple ideas that directly conflict with one another. Suppose someone is simultaneously confronted with conflicting realities in the real world rather than hypothetically. In that case, they are typically forced to pick one and discard the other so that the result ends well. Those who cannot realize or won't work out the contradiction, despite them occurring simultaneously in the perceived physical world, often believe they are the victims of continuous bad karma, but that is not true. They have not paid attention to the results long enough or intensely enough to discover the conflict. Often, this is considered bad luck, but it is merely due to conflicting ideas that are being held on to by them and driving them to act in ways that force the conflict to appear continually.

Some might be tempted to believe that karma is a net in which they are trapped. But what looks like a trap to one person might look like a safety net to another. And like all safety nets, this net is there for your benefit until you no longer need it.

Many religions wrongly believe human beings take their karma with them from one life to the next after death. These sects believe their followers will be blessed in the next life if they lived well in the last life, or will be cursed in the next life because of the mistakes they made in the past life. But karma is not like an anchor that you drag behind you from one life to the next, waiting to punish you for your misdeeds or reward you for a well-lived life. Karma is created and experienced by you exclusively within the transactional medium known as the perceived physical world, and karma exists only while you are awake.

To better understand the awakened mind, we must first differentiate between the awakened mind, the dreaming mind, and the deep sleeping mind. Imagine sitting in a completely dark movie theatre and looking up at the movie screen. The movie screen can be likened to your mind, the movie projected up on the screen can be likened to one of your three states of mind, and in this scenario, you, sitting comfortably in the theatre witnessing the movie, can be likened to that part of you which is deeper than thinking, awareness itself. As your awareness stares up at the screen, a double feature begins. The first movie is like your awakened mind. The projector projects up on the movie screen a very realistic fact-based movie with all the characters and objects you might see while awake. Then, when the first movie has finished, the next movie begins. The second movie is like your sleeping mind. This time, the projector projects a science fiction movie up on the screen that is rather odd and very unlike the first movie. It is at times very entertaining and at times very frightening, but you understand that it is not as realistic as the first movie. The third state of mind is deep sleep. This state of mind is not a movie at all. Instead, it is the time after the two movies have finished when the projector is turned off, and the screen and entire theatre go entirely into darkness. In this state of mind, you are still actively looking up at the screen but there is nothing to see on the screen. In deep sleep, the mind is overpowered by deep slumber. Instead of dreaming, the mind rests quietly within the body for a time, leaving your awareness with nothing to witness or experience. During all three states of mind and regardless of what was or was not projected upon the screen, you remained the witness of it all. Your awareness is the one that witnesses all three states of mind.

Now, as you reflect on your prior states of mind, you will likely realize that you have never experienced karma while you were dreaming or peacefully in deep sleep. This reveals that karma only exists within your awakened state of mind alone and not all three states of mind. Since karma appears to be attached only to your awakened mind and does not appear to be attached to either your dreaming state of mind or deep sleeping state of mind, it cannot be considered attached to your embodied soul. Thus, karma is restricted to only your awakened state of mind in this perceived physical life. It is your awakened state of mind that creates and experiences karma.

To better understand this, imagine you are playing a video game. In the video game, the actions of your avatar create actions and reactions that affect your avatar. But the moment you turn off the video game, the video game and its perceived effects on your avatar cease to be. It is easily understood that the video game only affects your avatar in the game, and cannot affect you. It is also easily understood that your avatar is the only one affected by the game and only when you actually play it. This is similar to what you experience during the awakened state of mind. Karma appears to exist and can only appear to affect you while your awakened state of mind is experiencing the perceived physical world. At the moment you begin to dream or go into deep sleep, the perceived physical world and the effects of karma cease to be.

When you push the save button on the imagined video game to be played later and then restart the game the next day, you do not have to suffer for mistakes you made the last time you played the game. Instead, you begin to play again with a fresh start. In the perceived physical world, like in the imagined video game, the only thing that comes back to the game is God's desire to continue the game.

In a similar way that your karma doesn't follow you from one life to the next, you don't take your knowledge with you when your body is considered to have died; you leave it here. It is easily understood that a person's avatar in a video game does not take the knowledge with it when the video game that they are playing is turned off. Instead, the advancements they achieved in the game are left within the game. It is similar to when you experience your perceived death. When your physical body dies, and you are believed to be dead, you leave your knowledge and advancements in the perceived physical world. This is because all of your thoughts and memories of your life's activities are exclusively the property of the living neurons within the brain, and they are lost when your perceived body dies. For some who have dementia, the thoughts and memories are lost while the person is still alive. But before they succumbed to dementia, they, like everyone else, could leave their written knowledge, shared knowledge, and documented experiences in the world.

For example, imagine the first man to have discovered fire. It must have been an absolute marvel to his friends and neighbors.

After witnessing this new invention, they would slowly begin to emulate his behavior and learn to start fires for themselves. By the time the man who invented fire got old and closed his eyes to pass away, most people in his tiny part of the world had learned to start fires and would share their newly acquired knowledge with others. In this way, he left his prior growth in his past life.

As the perceived physical world's knowledge became more advanced, many humans left their continually developing knowledge. They left their knowledge first in the spoken word and later progressed to writing. They advanced from drawings on cave walls to carving in stone, to writing on papyrus, and then began printing books. This ever-growing amount of knowledge had even improved to the point where it became available to them in multiple locations across the globe, such as bookstores and free libraries. The most recent advancement in leaving one's life's learning is a new storage space on the computer internet called the cloud. As of this writing, the world's learning and knowledge is cataloged, stored, and instantaneously accessible at the touch of a finger from anywhere on the planet. So, when human beings appear to be born into the perceived physical world, they do not need to remember anything; they only need to learn how to type or speak any question they may have into any one of several new and readily available devices, and the entire worlds combined knowledge magically becomes available to them. Knowledge remains in the perceived physical world and is available to each new generation of perceived human beings.

This has all been a part of what can be considered the process of growth and development of humanity. The first storehouse of knowledge was the brain cells. The next was the spoken word. The next was the written word. As of this writing, the more advanced storehouse of knowledge is an internet storage site known as "The Cloud." Each of these advancements acts as an ever-improving storage site for an ever-increasing level of knowledge about the perceived external experiential world, stored within the game of life and available to every human being as and when desired. The perceived experiential world is not designed to punish or reward; it is a transactional medium, a habitation within which to create and be entertained.

THE PURPOSE OF LIFE

It is all for God's habitation. Imagine if you suddenly realized that you were an infinite being. Where would you want to live? You likely wouldn't want to live in the darkness of space forever. And how would you design the place where you would live? The design and location would have to be the perfect place to exist for thousands, millions, billions, and even trillions of years at a time. There would have to be enough happening to occupy you and remain interesting for eternity. That could be a complex task to accomplish.

If it is difficult for humans to repeatedly see the same old movie, imagine how hard it would be for God to create a habitation that would entertain God forever. It is well known that humans are entertained by watching movies. They want to see images of a world they will likely never experience outside the movie theatre. They enjoy dramas, horror movies, action thrillers, murder mysteries, comedies, and more. Human beings find entertainment in a seemingly infinite variety of genres. They like to cry during sad movies, try to figure out the plot of mystery movies, scream in fear during horror movies, and laugh out loud during comedy movies. Regardless of what appears on the movie screen, they can sit safely in the theater or in the comfort of their favorite chair at home and enjoy the evening's entertainment. If someone tries to tell them how the movie ends before they can see the movie, the person that tells is called a spoiler because the one that told usually gives away the ending and spoils the other's ability to react to the movie in real-time while the movie is playing. They want to see the movie's plot unfold themselves. When they watch a horror movie, they are thrilled at the plot and the terrifying murders. They are so comfortable that they even complain if the blood or the screams aren't believable enough or the graphics appear substandard. Realism and new ideas make the latest movie worth watching.

It is similar to interactive video games. Human beings play video games to have an experience they cannot have outside of video games. Anyone who has ever played a video game wants the game they paid their hard-earned money for to be as exciting as possible, have the latest technology, be as realistic as possible, and have each level present more difficult and complex challenges. The more realistic the beasts, monsters, or enemy soldiers they must destroy or overcome in the game, the happier the player becomes.

This is where it gets interesting. God has everything because God is everything. So, what else could God desire if God is the entire perceived known and unknown universe itself? The answer is not what but who. God is everything and has everything, but God has no one to share it with. Even when one is everything and has everything, one can still be alone. We see simple parallels on a smaller scale in everyday life that reveal the basis of this desire. When a man grows up and has everything he needs, what is he still missing? Someone to share it with, a wife. When you get married, you don't marry something. You marry someone. When they get married and settle down, what are they missing? A family. When God created conscious beings, God didn't create a what; God created a who, someone with whom God could have a relationship.

When humans decide to have a child, they do so because of an innate desire to reproduce reflections of themselves in human form. After the child is born, the parent is much too old to be a child again, but the parent still can see the world as a child vicariously through their children's eyes. Although the parent is much too old to climb a tree, play a game of jump rope, or fight on a playground over a ball, the parent can indirectly recall the enjoyment of the activities as a child while they watch their children perform the activities. Similarly, God desired to create human beings and live indirectly through their experiences, only on a grander scale.

This is the beauty of God's creation, God's habitation, the perceived physical universe. In what has been called "The Beginning," it is said that God projected from within God's infinite self the seemingly infinite perceived physical universe, a multidimensional interactive reality composed of ever-changing material energy and structured by Karma. God also created an endless and ever-changing number of perceived conscious life forms, including human beings, said to have been created in God's own image, allowing God to experience God's creation through their perceived physical senses indirectly. This type of ever-changing three-dimensional video game is God's habitation.

Some wrongly believe that God must have forgotten his reality and is now living within the consciousness of human beings with a kind of memory loss. This is not true. Imagine playing a good video game. You decide which video game to play and then focus all your attention on the video game. You intentionally try to block out any other interruptions so that you can hopefully "Get into" the video game. Your desire is to completely immerse yourself without any distractions so that you can maximize your entertainment.

It can be seen in a similar way with God. When God projected the perceived physical universe into being, God became wholly immersed in the seemingly everchanging and infinite perceived universe. God, in this state, is immersed entirely in this three-dimensional game of sorts. If God were to become distracted by the totality of God's knowledge while witnessing the game, the game would likely lose its entertainment value quite rapidly. In a similar way that a human can desire to remain focused on a peaceful dream, a good book, or an entertaining videogame, God is doing something comparable on an entirely different scale.

Imagine two birds on the branch of a fruit tree. The first bird is far out on the branch eating fruit, while the second bird sits on the same branch near the tree trunk and watches as the first bird interacts with the tree's fruit. When the first bird eats a sour fruit, it becomes unhappy and frowns. When the first bird eats a sweet fruit, it becomes happy and smiles. The second bird nearest the tree trunk never eats any of the tree's fruit. The second bird instead lives vicariously through the experiences of the first bird farthest out on the branch.

It is like this with the perceived physical world all around you. While everything in the known and unknown universe is, in actuality, only God, the tree represents the material energy of the perceived physical world, including your own perceived physical form. The first bird farthest out on the branch represents the embodied souls of all conscious life forms, including human beings. The second bird closest to the tree trunk represents God, indirectly experiencing the infinite variety of its creation, including all perceived objects and the experiences of every conscious being. In this way, God remains the primary substance of everything, while the world and all conscious beings within God appear as different from God, even while being God at the same time. All sentient beings can then perceive themselves as existing autonomously with the karma from their actions, creating their own personal "Heaven" or "Hell," and yet have God existing as the reality within them, witnessing every perceived experience. God's creation is not only a place to be; it is the way to enjoy the beauty of being using one's own reflection.

Some think it is reasonable to ask why God would have created a world where the innocent suffer needlessly. They might enquire as to why a child is born only to die days later from starvation in its mother's arms. Questions like this are only reasonable if the person asking still sees the world as a wave rather than as ocean, as something more than an appearance within God. The simple fact that the question arose reveals that the inquirer is not yet grounded in the realization that there is no life or death for an infinite being within a perceived physical form. Think of waves in the ocean. It is their random beginning at various locations in the ocean that creates an individual set of challenges for each wave alone. Some waves appear to be born only yards from the beach and exist only for moments. Other waves appear to be born thousands of miles away from the beach and exist much longer. But all waves that appear to be born must eventually break on the shore, appearing to die before returning to their true nature, the ocean. Those who don't yet understand the eternal nature of the ocean focus instead on the temporary appearance of waves as they break and the fear it produces within them due to their ignorance.

The perceived physical world and the appearance of all its objects, joy, and suffering can be likened to the things that exist within a dream. The worlds that appear within dreams are random, and no two are the same. Some are fun, some are sad, some are tragic, some are terrifying, and some are disgusting. But all are only appearances within dreams.

CREATION

The idea of the creation of the universe is a complex concept that is difficult to imagine, let alone fully understand. One reason the concept of creation has been challenging to understand is the way in which scholars have historically approached the idea. Some scientists have postulated that creation is a specific point in time wherein a big bang brought everything into existence. Some religious scholars have postulated that creation is the first moment in a six-day period when God created the infinite universe from nothing. While many varied approaches have been used in humanity's effort to comprehend the actual creation process, when William Shakespeare said, "Life is but a dream," he may have been closest to the truth. To better understand precisely why Mr. Shakespeare was closer than most, we will employ a common-sense approach that will hopefully allow for greater accuracy.

Our common-sense approach will begin with imagining that we are looking at a chain on a bicycle. We can see from a close examination that the long chain is composed of smaller units called links. Each link is, in a very uniform way, a part of the whole chain. If we can understand the reality of a single part of the chain, one link, we should be able to extrapolate the reality of the entire chain reasonably. In this way, we don't have to address the entire chain; we can understand a part of the whole and then expand that knowledge to the entire chain.

Similarly, instead of attempting to understand the process of creation of the entire universe, let's just look at a tiny part of what everyone experiences very commonly in their everyday life and see if we can't extrapolate that tiny part into the information that might help us to understand the whole concept. Let us look at our little dreams. There are more times than most people can count when they experience periods of sleep in which they dream. For the dream state to occur, one must go into a state of relaxed slumber. In that state, the mind creates images within each individual that seem very real. Images of other people, places, and situations that seem incredibly real occur during the dream. From within themselves, the appearance of an entire world is created, and their minds become the stage. The dreamer is the material and efficient cause of a dream that appears real, but is not. The dreamer is the cause of the dream and the experiencer of the dream at the same time. The dream is not real, but the dreamer is. This dream state reveals that there is an external world that human beings believe is real and an internal world that they experience only within their minds as an imaginary world that is not considered real, like the external world.

Now, let us expand the concept to something much greater. It has been written in the different Abrahamic religions that God created human beings in God's image. If all of humanity were created in God's image, each human being would be similar to a single link in an infinitely larger chain known as God. According to the ancient Indian Philosopher and theologian Shankara, "God is both the material and the efficient cause through Maya, but not in reality. God has not become this universe, but this universe is not, and God is." This sounds very much like what every human has experienced in a dream.

Is it possible to intentionally create an image in the human mind when one is not dreaming? In a word, yes. It is commonly understood that the mind creates an image for every spoken word. For example, if I say the word elephant, an image of an elephant is instantaneously produced in my mind. This reveals that every spoken word creates an image to match the word. When anyone says the word monkey, the mind starts to create the image of a monkey. Try to stop thinking of a monkey; all that will happen is that more monkeys will appear over time. The mind is very good at adding and multiplying images.

Now, let us see how this might apply to the concept of the creation of the universe. The various Bibles from the Eastern and Western religions generally agree the universe was created or projected into being. More importantly, they say that it began with a word. The Apostle John in the Christian New Testament stated, "In the beginning was the Word, and the Word was with God, and the Word was God." It began with a word. In the Hebrew Torah, it states, "And God said..." Many Eastern religions agree. The Hindus have a sacred symbol that correlates to the sacred sound AUM. It is written in their texts that the sound AUM was present at the beginning of the universe. So, in a somewhat similar way that a little human being can create an internal image in themselves with the vibratory energy of a word from within themselves, God's vibratory energy or word could also cause or project an image within God. Since God is all, which is much, much bigger and infinitely more complex than a human being, to say the least, it also makes sense that the image would appear larger, even as large as the apparent infinite universe.

Now, let us look at the same concept from another perspective: a single wave in the ocean. For a single wave to exist in the ocean, there must be a cause. For the purpose of this discussion, the cause will be the energy of the wind. As the wind sweeps across the ocean's surface, the wind energy attempts to separate the molecules in the ocean. The water molecules resist the wind by transferring the energy of the wind to adjacent water molecules. This energy transfer causes the ocean surface to rise and appear as a wave. As the wave appears on the surface, time and space become measures of the wave. In this way, causation, space, and time exist almost as shadows of the wave. Something caused the wave to exist over a specific period of time and within a particular space. But once the energy that acted upon the wave ceases to exist, so does the time and space, as they were entirely dependent upon the wave for their existence. They cannot exist without the wave. The only thing that actually existed in the ocean the entire time, was that which already existed: the ocean. The wave was nothing more than a different appearance of the ocean. Similarly, the universe was not created per se. It was projected into being in waveform and is merely an appearance within God. The cause is God, and the perceived material universe is the effect within God.

Let us look at something as familiar as a chair in order to look at the example of the wave from yet another angle. We will go backward from the effect (the universe) to the cause (God), starting with a chair. At first glance, we see only a chair. But if we look closer, we will see that the chair is, in reality, a combination of molecules that appear as wood. If we look even closer, we will see that the molecules are, in reality, a combination of atoms that appear as molecules. If we look even closer, we will see that the atoms are, in reality, a combination of protons, electrons, and neutrons that appear as individual atoms. If we look even closer, we will see that the protons and neutrons are a combination of quarks that appear as atomic nuclei. If we look even closer, we will see that the quarks and are elementary particles composed of a combination of what has been theorized to be something similar to transcendental string-like objects within a multidimensional quantum field that, when acted upon by some as of yet unknown force, vibrate in wave-like patterns or frequencies until they undergo a process of super-compactification and eventually appear as quarks. So, the chair's cause is some unknown energy that acts upon the subatomic quantum field, creating vibrations within it; something like the vibration that can be created with a word.

On an aside and equally important, the seemingly infinite subatomic quantum field cannot exist outside of or independent of space and time. Space and time are manifested from the motion of the subatomic quantum field throughout the time it is in motion in response to awareness as it observes the field.

In the human microcosm, there cannot be a single wave of thought that is unconditioned by name and form. If it is true that the macrocosm is built throughout by the same plan, this kind of conditioning by name and form must also be in the plan of the entire universe. So, let's look at the creation of the perceived universe again. It should now seem logical that Shankara might have come very close to the truth one thousand four hundred years ago when he said,

"God is both the material and the efficient cause through Maya, but not in reality. God has not become this universe, but this universe is not, and God is." Shakespeare put a finer point on it when he said, "Life is but a dream."

GOOD AND EVIL

The different religions tend to interpret the meaning of good and evil differently. Some religions consider good and evil to represent opposing forces. To them, good represents light, virtue, righteousness, morality, and dignity, while evil represents darkness, depravity, corruption, and destruction. In Christianity, the Angel symbolizes goodness, bowing to God, the source of all that is good, and the Devil symbolizes all that is bad, rebelling against God's will. Hindus view good and evil as two sides of the same coin, each playing an essential role in deciding your fate in future lives. Most of humanity, at some point and regardless of religious affiliation, will either be grateful for what they consider good or believe that they are suffering due to that which they consider bad. All of these interpretations of good and evil are wrong. Good and evil exist only in the mind, are a product of flawed perceptions, and are false concepts. There are three reasons why Good and evil represent nothing more than flawed perceptions within the illusory world.

Good and evil are false concepts first because they do not exist as real things. Rather, they exist only as interdependent terms used to measure human beings' perceptions within their perceived physical world. What human beings consider good depends upon what they consider evil to be. Likewise, evil depends upon what human beings consider good to be. Since good and evil are used to measure one another, they cannot be regarded as separate. If you were to try to make one stand-alone without the other, you would lose the way to measure it, and the term would no longer have any meaning. If you try to make evil stand entirely by itself without good to measure it, you would no longer be able to recognize it as evil. Since good and evil do not exist independently as a sort of thing, good and evil can only be considered a degree of measure, like the difference between hot and cold or black and white.

The second reason good and evil are false concepts is that good and evil can be changed by the circumstances or the results that they produce. What can appear evil under one circumstance may be considered good under another circumstance. What one might see as good in one case may appear evil if the conditions and results were different. Water is good when used to quench your thirst, but it is evil when it drowns someone. Fire is good when it keeps someone from freezing in the winter, but evil when it burns down a village. If a soldier returned from the battlefield after killing 200 men from his enemy's country, you would call him good, but if the same man killed a single person in his own country, you would call him evil. In this way, your perceptions of good and evil were not based on fire, water, or the killer. Your perceptions of good and evil were based upon the results that they produced.

The third reason Good and evil are false concepts is that the measure of good and evil can be changed based on one's relative position. If a man stepped over a starving person to give food to a different person who was also starving, the person receiving the food would see the man as good, while the person who was stepped over and left to remain hungry would see the man as evil. Or if a man caught a fish to feed his family, his family would see the man as good, while a vegetarian person opposed to eating meat would see the man as evil. Cases like this represent nothing more in reality than a kind of subtle narcissism in the person who considers themselves elevated to such a degree above their neighbors that they feel entitled to be the judge of other's actions.

Many religions are fervent supporters of the concept of good and evil. They often intentionally conflate their church's current cultural and moral standards with good and evil as they judge humanity's interactions. For example, if someone in their community gives or does something their religion believes is good for their religion, they are considered good. If someone in their community does something that their religion believes takes away from or harms anyone in their religion, they are evil. Religions, in protecting their ideologic narrative, often refuse to accept or admit that the nature of man is to vacillate between what is considered good and evil. At times, every man can appear evil, and at times, every man can appear good depending on the moment their actions were viewed. But man is never only one or the other. Rather, man is constantly making what they consider the best decision possible using their available knowledge at that time. Despite this, these religions do not judge them by their intent, level of knowledge, or decision-making skills that led to the action. Instead, they are routinely judged exclusively by the outcome of their action at a specific point in time.

This judgmental aspect of these religions inevitably creates a kind of narcissism that quickly descends into a form of control as each religion establishes different ideas of punishment and reward for countless activities. The more the religion perceives the one being judged as doing good for the church, themselves, and others, the better their reward, not now but in the future. The more the religion perceives the one being judged as taking away from the religion, the group, or injuring others, the greater the punishment, now and in the future. As the religion grows in power over its followers, it often shepherds their followers into a kind of dystopia. It also alienates the rest of humanity, as those who are from different cultures are usually quite unaware of their zealous neighbors' stringent rules and religious standards. In one country, something that may be considered moral or good may be regarded as immoral or evil in another. Those countries that do not fit into one another's standard of moral goodness typically become judged as lesser humans, evil, or even devils for their different morality. In these cases, these religions, over time, first expect and then require their neighbor countries or sometimes groups they encounter in their own country to accept their cultural norms. Those who refuse to accept these standards may be forced by the penalty of death to succumb to them. The Christian New Testament reveals an example of this authoritarian aspect of religion. Romans 13 states, "3 For rulers hold no terror for those who do right, but for those who do wrong. Do you want to be free from fear of the one in authority? Then do what is right, and you will be commended. 4 For the one in authority is God's servant for your good. But if you do wrong, be afraid, for rulers do not bear the sword for no reason. They are God's servants, agents of wrath to bring punishment on the wrongdoer. 5 Therefore, it is necessary to submit to the authorities, not only because of possible punishment but also as a matter of conscience." Innumerable wars, horrific atrocities, and destruction at every level have been observed over thousands of years in the name of religion's ideas of good and evil.

You must understand that when humans attempt to judge anything from their standpoint, they will never be able to use the concept of good or evil as an accurate measure, not only because their knowledge is limited and imperfect, but because good and evil are false concepts. Do not blame God for what you consider evil or thank God for what you consider good. You should instead see God as impartial as the sun and realize that your ideas about good and evil exist only in your mind, are a product of your creation, are false, and must be removed from you by you.

SUFFERING

Human beings are not subjected to suffering by God; human beings create their suffering. Some suffer because of what they choose to recall from the past. Others suffer because of how they visualize the future.

The first cause of suffering occurs because of what they choose to recall from their past. To see the point a bit more clearly, imagine billowing clouds rolling slowly overhead from east to west. Imagine that every other cloud is labeled differently. The first cloud is labeled happiness; the second cloud is labeled suffering; the third cloud is labeled happiness; the fourth cloud is labeled suffering, and so on, for all the clouds that pass overhead in a human being's lifetime. Those who claim all of life is suffering have simply chosen to recall only the clouds labeled suffering and have forgotten or refused to recall all the clouds labeled happiness. They claim that all of life is suffering, yet they find themselves able to be happy occasionally. If all of life is indeed suffering and there is no happiness at all, then why would any reasonable person continue to live in such a horrific place? The reality is that they do experience happiness more often than they are willing to admit. They have merely chosen not to appreciate the happy moments and instead prefer to focus exclusively on their past suffering.

Some will tell others around them that reminding themselves of their past suffering is what keeps them from reliving it. Those are the ones who become unable to move forward in their perceived physical world because of their mistaken logic. Their minds become so full of negative memories from their past that they become terrified of change and find themselves frozen in life, unable to move onward. They hold on to their memories of past suffering to justify their current suffering. They wear their suffering like a badge of honor. They try to use their suffering as evidence that finding peace or prosperity in this perceived life is impossible. Some even try to convince themselves and others that it is God's will that they suffer. They show their suffering proudly to others in an effort to convince anyone who will listen that their lifetime of suffering makes them somehow more knowledgeable, more special, more deserving of pity now, or more deserving of praise at a later date in time.

Before we explore the second cause of suffering, we should consider why there can be no suffering in the present. It is because there is no now; there is no present. All of your perceptions of the world around you are false, and all of your perceptions of time within which you experience those perceptions are also false. There is no now. All of the moments that you believe are happening now are not in reality happening now at all. Instead, they are streaming moments in time, like all-encompassing pictures you are witnessing, organizing, and reacting to. They are also moments in history.

What you think you are currently seeing, feeling, hearing, tasting, or smelling does not go directly to you, the awareness. The information you experience has taken time to get from where it interacted with your body, through your nervous system, to your brain; more time for your brain to process it, and even more time for your mind to deliver it to you. It may have taken only three one-thousandths of one second, but that is still some time. So, what you think you are currently seeing is, in reality, only what was happening moments ago. You are experiencing and reacting to an illusory past.

The second cause of suffering is found in the way human beings choose to visualize the future. To better understand this, it is necessary first to learn the difference between faith and doubt because both forms of willpower come into existence and remain in existence only with each individual's approval and acceptance.

Every human being is continually affected by an ongoing internal struggle when they attempt to look to the future. It is the struggle between faith and doubt that occurs entirely in the human being's mind. Faith and doubt have one thing in common. They both ask you to believe something is going to happen that you have yet to experience. When the mind offers doubt, you must choose to agree or disagree with the thought. If you choose to agree with doubt, you have surrendered your faith because no one and nothing can take away your faith; you must give it away.

Doubt results from humans' mistaken sense of isolation and misunderstanding of the perceived physical world. Doubt convinces them to give up their faith and make desperate attempts to obtain peace through the perceived physical world, using their body's physical senses. This selfish desire, having a strong will to live as its basis, seeks what it believes is desirable, even if it is sometimes death and always leads to suffering. A life that is not free from worldly desire and passion is always involved with distress and suffering. If your mind offers doubt, but you refuse doubt and instead choose faith, then you have agreed with faith. Holding on to faith, you will focus on the best-case scenario. That best-case scenario will then play out over time and become your reality, ultimately creating the reward of peace.

With faith, human beings, regardless of the perceived physical world's effects on their senses, remove thoughts filled with doubt, utilize self-restraint, and act in ways that they believe are appropriate. With the restraint of the self that can be governed, they attain calmness. In calmness, they experience peace. In this perceived physical world, it is your own choices that will move you toward either peace or suffering.

Imagine faith and doubt were opposite directions you could choose to travel on the same path. If you travel in one direction, it will be called the faithful path. If you travel away from faith in the opposite direction, it will be called the doubtful path. Even though the paths are on the same road, they will appear to be different because they lead in opposite directions and to different results. If a person chooses the faithful path, it will eventually lead them to peace. In the other direction is the doubtful path. If the person chooses the doubtful path, it will ultimately lead them to suffering. Often, the two different directions on the same path may closely resemble one another; however, it is the outcome of your actions that will reveal to you whether or not you are, in fact, on the faithful path. Did your action bring you peace or suffering? In this way, peace and suffering remind you of your chosen direction.

Imagine a hermit living in a cave shut off from the outside world. The only way the hermit can get an idea of the external world is through probing with his five fingers (the body's five senses) outside through a small hole, low in the cave, near the ground. When the hermit pokes his five fingers through the hole to feel what is outside, he can only receive the tiniest amount of information from the external world. The hermit must then attempt, on his own, to deduce what that small amount of information means. As the hermit reaches through the hole to feel, he feels something furry brush by softly and attempts to imagine what it is. From his perspective, the hermit's senses tell him it could either be the top of a harmless rabbit or the bottom of a terrible bear. This is an excellent example of misunderstanding. Just as there is no way the hermit can understand what is actually around him by placing his hand out of the cave and into the immeasurable and unknown universe, there is no way that human beings can understand everything around them with such limited tools as their sense organs.

Now, based upon the limited information the hermit received and his integration of this new information with his past experiences, the hermit will attempt to come up with his interpretation of what he believes he experienced and create his best guess about what is out there. This reveals that the hermit's interpretation is less about what his senses experienced and more about his perceptions. What he felt with his senses was likely not a bear or a rabbit. Despite this, with this best guess, the hermit will attempt to predict what he believes he experienced and then create and implement what he believes will be the most appropriate response to this new perceived reality.

This imaginary scenario is the kind of thing that separates the most wonderful human beings from the most horrible human beings. Each human being's actions are based entirely upon their misunderstanding and misinterpretation of the perceived physical world. If the hermit chooses doubt, he will begin to believe it is a terrible bear; he has chosen the worst-case scenario. His doubt will then create fear within him that he may be in danger, and from that point of view, the hermit will lose his sound judgment and choose actions that will ultimately end in suffering. If the hermit chooses faith, he will believe it is a harmless rabbit. Armed with the faith that his thoughts of bears must be due solely to his misunderstanding, the hermit uses his good judgment to choose actions that ultimately result in peace. In this illusory world, there is no way at this time to truly understand the external reality you so firmly believe you experience. You must choose between faith and doubt with your current ignorance and limitations.

Agreeing with faith results in your never-ending desire to forge on, deciding never to give up, regardless of anything, until your idea, dream, goal, or mission becomes a reality. Agreeing with doubt results in you trying half-heartedly and then giving up. This is, in reality, what human beings think is the devil. There is no devil; there is only doubt. What you believe is the devil is merely the doubts created by your mind, acting as the voice inside you, convincing you that you cannot, and reminding you of your past failures. It is the voice that tells you it can never be achieved. It is the voice that eats away at your self-confidence. If you believe something is not working out for you, it is simply your doubts.

All of your perceptions about the world you live in are mistaken. Your current perceptions of what you are and who you are only represent misperceptions and misunderstanding that you have placed upon yourself through your ignorance and past doubts.

The bad omens and bad luck you believe in are, in reality, nothing more than your doubts. It is only your doubts telling you those bad things could happen, and you surrendering to those doubts that allow them to happen. In fact, any thought created by you that attempts to convince you that you do not have the right to exist in peace is false. All of your prior suffering has been the result of your past doubts.

This perceived existence can sometimes feel like being on a ship at sea caught in a violent storm. The human being without faith may feel utterly alone in the storm, and the ride will seem like a terrifying nightmare. As his faith is pulled away by his doubts and roaming senses, he will allow his faith to be carried away by the fierce wind and waves. But the wise human beings will exercise their faith that God exists all around them and will see the storm only as an event they do not yet understand. They will look with amazement at God's creation and experience peace.

Some believe that the evil in this perceived physical world is the cause of suffering, but they are wrong. As we have already discussed, your ideas about good and evil exist only in your mind, are also a product of your creation, and are false concepts. Good and evil represent nothing more than your flawed perceptions in an Illusory world.

Some wrongly believe that the destruction they observe in the perceived physical world is the cause of suffering, but their perceptions of the world they think they live in are false. Destruction and creation in the perceived physical world are only ideas that rely upon each other, and one's limited understanding creates both. The material energy of the entire perceived physical world is in constant motion and a constant state of change. If you look at a large rock, you will believe you are looking at a very solid and unchanging object. But that is not true. The atoms that make up the composition of the large rock have electrons that are all moving in circular patterns at the speed of light. So, the rock and even the mountain you have seen before as solid and unchanging can also be seen as subatomic fields of energy that are continually in motion and constantly changing. From that perspective, the mountain is never the same object from one moment to the next. In fact, everything in the entire perceived physical world is in constant motion, and all of the objects you believe you see are not only changing, but their forms are continually coming into and out of existence, just at different speeds. The mountain you see today will not be there ten million years from now, and volcanoes that have not yet erupted will build the future mountains. This constant change that appears to you as cycles of creation and destruction is a natural part of the perceived physical world. For example, in the spring, a seed is planted; creation. In the fall, the wheat is cut down; destruction. The grain is turned into bread; creation. The bread is consumed; destruction. The bread builds your body; creation. The body dies; destruction.

You believe you see creation and destruction happening all around you, and yet through all of it, you, the witness of it all, remain entirely unchanged and untouched by it. Since that internal unchanging aspect of you is separate from all this creation and destruction, how can you possibly suffer from it? You cannot. Only your doubts create your suffering, and you holding on to the belief that the objects in the perceived physical world are somehow connected to you, that they are a part of you, is what allows your suffering to remain.

When you stumble and break a toe, you will begin to want to believe that you are suffering. At that moment, ask yourself, who is suffering? Your toe has experienced an injury, and the pain receptors send messages related to the trauma to your brain cells. But that does not mean that your embodied soul was injured. It was not. The injury was isolated to only your toe and did not affect your embodied soul. You could even surgically remove the toe, and the result would have absolutely no effect on your embodied soul. You will remain the same conscious being after the procedure. The fact is that the perceived physical world cannot affect you. It is merely your doubts that cause your suffering because it is you who clings to them, refusing to choose faith instead.

Imagine you see a man sitting on the bank of a river. As the man sits, he sees two different things floating by in the river. Faith floats by. Doubt also floats by. As each floats by, the man gets to decide what he wants to swim out to, grab, and bring back to the bank of the river. Regardless of which is chosen, when the man carries it back to the bank of the river, he mistakenly wraps it around himself tightly and begins to convince himself that it is him. If he swims out and grabs onto faith, he will end up saying, "I am peaceful." If he swims out and grabs onto doubt, he will end up saying, "I am suffering." But the truth is that those things the man was holding on to were in his possession, but those things were not him. Faith, which led to peace, or doubt, which led to suffering, were simply things the man decided to hold on to. He could release them back into the river at any moment and let them go. The man has the authority and ability to swim out and grab a different item at any time.

The mere fact that human beings are incapable of having the same continual experience where they are always peaceful or always suffering serves as further evidence that the river of this perceived physical life continually offers new opportunities to choose faith over doubt. It is you who is constantly making different choices about what to grab onto and what to let go of. Faith, which leads to peace, or doubt, which leads to suffering, are yours to choose, but they are not you. They are merely items you may choose to pull out of the river of life that allow you to experience the illusory world as you desire. You can overcome suffering at any time by choosing faith over doubt at every opportunity. When all the people in the world continually draw faith from the river of life instead of doubt, suffering will cease to exist.

ACCIDENTS AND ERRORS

Your thoughts of past accidents and errors are merely the product of your mind's manipulation of the past, not reality. In this discussion, I will reveal three reasons that prove all of your memories of past accidents and errors are false and, therefore, must not be trusted. Once you understand these concepts, letting go of your past accidents and errors should be natural and allow you to move closer to the experience of the real peace that has always been available.

First, your thoughts about past accidents and errors are false because your mind presents the past as you want to see it rather than as it actually was. Your past is nothing more than what you have chosen to remember from your perspective, your personal point of view. For example, you remember your mother in a very specific light. You remember her as your mother, and all of your memories contain memories of her from that perspective. But your father remembers the same woman as his wife, and her parents remember the same woman as their daughter. When looking at the exact same person, each of these people saw the same person from entirely different perspectives. They did not see the woman as she was; they only saw her as they wanted to see her.

The second reason your thoughts about past accidents and errors are false is that your mind changes the way you see the past based on your emotions each time you review the past. Imagine you are in a relationship with a very close friend. You are happy to be in the relationship when everything is going well in your friendship. But when you and your friend begin discussing something you seriously disagree about, and you begin to argue, your anger at that moment instantly changes all of your thoughts about that person, and your anger changes the way you see the past. After parting in anger, all you can remember are the bad times, the earlier disagreements, and the fighting. That is all you can see. You thank God that the friendship has ended, and you kick yourself for having made them a friend in the first place. But when your friend calls you later, apologizes, and makes up with you, all of your emotions and memories are once again immediately changed. You begin to happily recall all of the reasons you became friends in the first place. From this newly changed perspective, you even start to convince yourself that the bad moments, like the last argument, are the very thing that helped you to have such a wonderful and rich friendship now. Your mind even attempts to convince you that the bad times helped you build such a strong relationship. The truth is that all of your thoughts about the past are false because they are constantly being changed by your mind, depending on your feelings at each moment of your life.

The third reason your thoughts of past accidents and errors are all false is that each time your mind mentally reviews one of your past thoughts, you look at the thought through the lens of the current you rather than see it as you experienced it then. When you made a mistake or experienced failure as a younger person, your perspective or circumstance at the time you failed or made a mistake was conditioned and affected by your mental limitations, lack of understanding, lack of objectivity, and lack of insight at that specific time. As an older person, everything about you has changed. You have fewer mental limitations, more understanding, and deeper insight. Looking at your past memories of accidents and errors from the perspective of the current you is, in reality, only an exercise in adding harsh judgments and reorganizing a past that you cannot change into something worse than what it actually was. It is an exercise in being cruel to yourself for your lack of understanding, lack of insight, and lack of ability in your past. Each time the memory is reviewed, it is again changed by the new, more mature you and is always changed incorrectly. The memory is at that moment, once again, only what you can understand or believe at that moment, and not really the past at all. The truth is that all of your memories of the past are false and, therefore, must not be trusted. Your thoughts of past accidents and errors should simply be treated as false information and be let go.

Fools hold on to their past accidents and errors, thinking that those memories will help them in the future, but that is not true. Holding on to past accidents and errors only takes up room in the conscious mind, which can be very dangerous. By thinking about your past, you may become your own worst enemy. If you look back at your past, you may unknowingly focus more on the bad memories than the good and begin to wrongly conclude that the majority of your life was spent suffering. This is a lie, and when allowed by you to grow, it will negatively affect your future decisions. If you allow your mind to continually bombard you with negative memories from your past, eventually, your faith will surrender to doubt. Once you have surrendered your faith, you have given up. Nothing good can come from dwelling on your past accidents and errors. Dwelling on them is focusing on situations and events that can never be changed.

Dwelling on past accidents and errors can poison your mind just as toxins can poison your body. If a doctor sees that a patient cannot naturally remove toxins from their body, the doctor will treat the patient to help them remove their toxins. The doctor is not surprised or upset that the body produced the toxins. The doctor is only concerned when the body cannot let them go naturally. It is the same with your past. It is not abnormal for bad things to have happened in the past, such as experiencing accidents or making mistakes. It is only unhealthy if they get stuck inside of you and are not released by you.

As we have already discussed, fools will say that being reminded of past accidents and errors is the very thing that prevents them from reliving them. Those humans have become unable to move forward in their perceived physical world because of their mistaken logic. Their minds are so full of negative memories from their past that they become terrified of change and the uncertainty of the unknown, and they give up their faith. Instead of acting in ways that create peace, they use their past to justify their doubts and the resultant suffering. They wear their suffering like a badge of honor. They try to use their suffering as evidence that finding peace or prosperity in this perceived life is impossible. Some even try to convince themselves and others that it is God's will that they suffer. They show their suffering proudly to others in an attempt to convince anyone who will listen that their doubt and the resultant suffering make them somehow more knowledgeable, unique, or deserving of God's praise at a later date in time.

But you were not born to suffer. You were born so that you could interact with and experience this perceived world in any way you desire. You have the right to expect and achieve real peace. If God is on your side, then what or who could ever stop you but you? The answer is nothing and no one, for when God is on your side, nothing and no one can stand against God except you. It is you who wields the power to sabotage your peace. One way you do this is by holding on to past accidents and errors.

The more you reflect on the reality that all of your memories of past accidents and errors are false and, therefore, must not be trusted, the more you will begin to effortlessly remove them from your mind as and when they arise. Throw out all thoughts of past accidents and errors the same way you would throw out anything else that has no value, regardless of the temptation, and never pick them back up again. Instead, fill the same mental space with forgiveness of self and others, dreams of the future, or experiences in the present moment.

RELIGION

Throughout history, as ancient humans developed into larger and larger social groups, a few wise men and women combined their revelations with their knowledge and insight. Each created a uniquely divine message suited to their listener's spiritual development and culture at that specific period in time. This is the foundation of different religions. Water's name may change from "river" to "lake" to "sea" to "rain" due to its form, but the water remains the same in its substance. Similarly, religions may appear different from place to place and group to group in their form, but they will remain essentially the same in substance.

Religions do not fight over the existence of God. They battle over God's different attributes. Each religion attempts to limit God to their understanding, and this is their mistake. Attempting to define God as anything less than incomprehensible and eternal, the subject of all reality, beyond speech and concepts, the one true reality, is to fail to define God adequately. Those who have chosen to fight over the different aspects or forms of God fail to recognize the more profound truth and are lost. The wise are willing to seek out the essential truth of God throughout all religions. Until all religions can begin to understand that God can be seen through a monotheistic, pantheistic, and polytheistic view, at the same time, they will be destructive by their very nature.

Those filled with misunderstanding will speak in lofty language, delighted by the words of their Bibles and church, declaring, "There is no other truth!" Those are distracted souls who desire to learn one way, refusing to look further than what is before them. Their minds are closed, and their spiritual growth has stopped because they are preoccupied with their ritualistic acts and defending their religion's dogma. Those whose desire to learn has been carried away by their religion will offer themselves to their deities and waste their time following their rules without realizing they are ruled not by the deities but by their worldly nature.

Those who have failed to interpret their bible correctly will hold their books above them and exclaim that there is no other way. They are like fools who have found the wrong map to heaven. They spent countless hours memorizing every millimeter of their map, believing it reveals the only way to heaven. Unable to see that heaven has been all around them and even within them the entire time, they remain distracted by a book to nowhere.

Most religions have become more extreme and more polarized over time. On one side of the two extremes, there are religions that consider themselves to be conservative. These religions only subscribe to a very literal and restricted translation of their specific text. They demand that their followers accept their text as the only eternal, infallible, sacred truth, and they must voluntarily give up their right to question either the text or their leader's interpretations of the text. Their leaders are so egotistical with regard to their piety and perceived level of knowledge related to their version of religion that they flatly dismiss any objections to their point of view at best as stupidity and at worst as malice on the part of those they deem less educated, less important, or less a part of their clique. Followers of these conservative religions have stopped trying to learn with an open mind and instead have chosen follow their leaders mindlessly. When given new information, regardless of the source, they often oppose any facts that differ from their leader's conservative translation of their text and instead choose only that which they believe will strengthen their position. They look at anyone who differs from their view as wicked or immoral.

On the other side, there are religious groups that call themselves liberal. These loosely structured religious sects tend to be inherently unstable because they lack religious substance in their organization. Over time, they usually allow themselves to degenerate into either a social or political group. Followers of these liberal religious groups often spend their time involved in social or political activism defending the latest cause. These followers usually avoid physical contact with conservative religious seekers but maintain social contact by intermittently visiting like-minded individuals at rallies, on alternative religious websites, political organizations, or rehabilitation groups. In the name of what they consider religious freedom, they feed their idle curiosity with an endless succession of what can best be described as intellectual arguments against whatever they read or see. With them, ideas that are different from theirs or are offered by religious seekers are treated like an affliction. They gain a kind of nervous excitement when they treat new or different ideas with their long-held negativism in a similar way that a bully in school would try to trip another child walking peacefully by with a lunch plate full of food. These are the kinds that troll religious websites anonymously under ridiculous pseudonyms that they give to themselves. Religion with these people is a sort of intellectual self-indulgence, and that is the limit of their devotion. Religious liberals claim to have the same kind of love as other religious seekers. The only difference is how they direct their passion, which drives the religious seeker to do good works, while the religious liberal does harm. Religious seekers love others, while religious liberals love themselves.

Because of this, it is difficult, if not impossible, for the ordinary person seeking religious knowledge, with a reasonable degree of intelligence and an open mind, to become a part of any religious organization. The conservative religious groups display commendable levels of love for those who share their ideals while hating anyone who doesn't subscribe to them. In contrast, the liberal religious groups act as narcissistic political and social clubs that prefer the role of critic over the role of contributor. It is essential to exercise caution in the presence of religious conservatives and religious liberals. Do not argue with them. Do not interfere with them. Leave them alone to pursue their own path. One whose knowledge is more advanced should not disturb those whose knowledge is less complete.

Suppose you desire to learn more about a specific religion beyond their texts. In that case, care must be taken when interacting with their religious group's leadership and or followers to differentiate between religious extremists and religious moderates. Religious extremists like religious conservatives and religious liberals have historically done more harm than good. At their best, these religious groups prevent the individual's natural development. At their worst, these extreme religious groups mislead everyone, cause division and hate, and lead to horrible atrocities. There is an old story, " Once a mosquito settled gently upon a man's head. The man's friend, in an effort to kill the mosquito, hit the mosquito so hard that he killed both the mosquito and the man." Some religion's remedy of what they consider evil seems to suggest a similar course of action. It is best to avoid prolonged contact with religious extremists.

Instead, connect with moderate religious churches, synagogues, temples, or organizations. Religious moderates will help lift you up rather than knock you and others down. They are more interested in revelation than their revenue. Religious moderates are the ones who help their followers focus on the beauty of their true nature and identify the perfection within them. Moderate religious organizations help their followers intellectually see the heaven around them and within them and help to create heaven on earth within their communities. These groups' teachings and texts do not conflict with peace, love, compassion, and kindness toward all. If there is no moderate religious group near you, study everything available. Listen to those who inspire you and meditate on what you have experienced. There are innumerable books on philosophy and theology, as well as numerous bibles of the world, that have very valuable information within them. They can keep you learning for a lifetime. Even though the ancient Bibles and texts were written for a specific audience at a particular time, they have beautiful truths you can discover within their pages. Religion is between you and God; let no one and nothing come between you. For if you are genuinely seeking God, then you can rest assured that the grace of God is seeking you.

BE HEALTHY

You possess everything you need for this life experience. The physical attributes you believe you possess are quite sufficient to exist peacefully in this perceived physical world. While your body is yours but not you, your body is the temple, the tool, the avatar that allows you to integrate into the perceived physical world and interact with it. The care and management of your physical frame is an essential aspect of integrating into the perceived physical world because, without your optimal health and state of being, you will be unable to achieve the peace you are entitled to in this perceived life.

Your perceived physical body is temporarily yours and is designed to serve your needs. Not the other way around. If you had a favorite old shirt that was very dear to you, you would wear it, but you wouldn't spend your valuable time trying to make it happy. It is a shirt to be worn, a useful object, but not an object that controls you. The shirt is there to serve your needs. It is your happiness that is important when you surround yourself with it. Similarly, you do not live to make your body happy. Your body is an object like the shirt and similarly surrounds you like the shirt, but it is not you. Living to make your body happy is a way to deprive yourself of the real peace you are entitled to because you will be serving at the pleasure of an object rather than requiring the object to serve you. It will inevitably result in suffering.

The desires of your body are as transient as the clouds that come and go in the sky. As the clouds move into and out of your view over a short time, so will the desires of your body. If you can be patient enough to watch your desires come and go, like you do with the clouds in the sky, without being moved by your desires, you will become your body's master.

You may gain control of your body as and when you desire. Imagine your body's senses are like five large dogs, and you have been assigned the task of taking them all for a walk. Your intellectual determination is like the leash. As you attempt to walk the dogs in the direction of your choosing, one dog may want to run east towards the lake, one dog may wish to run west towards a field of grass, one dog may become tired and want to rest, one dog may want to run south after a squirrel, and one dog may have just been stung by a bee and want to run in any direction, as long as it is away from the bee. Without holding tightly to the leash, the dogs would struggle as they all attempt to go off in different directions. Being tied together by the leash, the most muscular dog would drag the rest of the dogs along with it at any one time. Similarly, the human body and its senses are tempted by desires. The body may want to eat more than it requires, rest more than it needs, be reckless, or take alcohol or chemicals that will make it temporarily make it feel better, regardless of the injuries that will result. If the body and its senses, like the dogs, are held tightly by the leash and are controlled by your intellectual determination to be healthy, the desires will subside in less time than you think and allow you to be in charge of your body's direction again. If you utilize self-restraint in managing your physical frame, you will guide your body, and there will be no trouble. Where there is self-restraint, there will be peace.

However, suppose you allow doubts to remain about becoming and staying healthy or create conflicts to achieving a healthy state. In that case, you will have given up control of the leash and will not be able to achieve or maintain your optimal state of health. If you sit around all day, overeat, eat a lousy diet, take drugs or alcohol, smoke, or place yourself in constantly stressful or harmful situations, you have given up your determination to be healthy, and your optimal health will not be achieved.

Imagine a human being who suffers from alcoholism or any other drug addiction. At first, the drug makes their body feel much better. But when the drug wears off, the body experiences severe anxiety and painful physical withdrawals. This is when the body and mind attempt to convince the awareness within that they should take more drugs to stop the anxiety, pain, and suffering of the withdrawal. With addictions like this, it becomes a battle between the body/mind and the intellect. If the person allows the body and mind to be in control of the decision, then they have given in to the pain of withdrawal, and they will allow their body to consume more drugs. This is precisely the time that a vicious cycle will begin, leading inevitably to illness, suffering, and, sadly, sometimes even death. But if, when the body tells the mind that it needs more drugs, the person takes control of the leash with their intellect and determination, they will regain control of their body and lead the body away from injury and towards optimal health. Without control of your body, you will not reach your optimal state of being.

You must be determined to manage and assist your body in maintaining the optimal function of its design. When you intellectually make decisions about your health from the perspective of the awareness within, it is possible, regardless of the environment or your current level of health, to achieve your optimal state of health. Remember this when you are making decisions about your health. It will help you to make better decisions. For example, you must be determined to choose intellectually when considering food choices. The food you have consumed thus far is the material from which your physical body was manufactured, and the food you choose from now on is the material out of which your physical body will be maintained. Remember, the materials you receive through your food into your perceived physical body go a long way in determining your physical and mental constitution. Therefore, you must be determined to educate yourself on the best food available and prioritize purchasing and consuming that food to ensure it receives the attention it deserves.

The cells in your body respond to you. When you make a decision, it is picked up by the cells of the nervous system. The nervous system then acts as the body's master controller and relays your decision to the cells in your body as and when needed, forcing them into action at a cellular level. Simply decide to touch an object, and your entire body will respond by moving toward the object and touching it. When you choose to go for a walk, your body will stand up in preparation because the moment you decide to walk, billions of living cells in your body will follow your command. Similarly, when you make conscious decisions about your health, you are making plans at a cellular level. Deciding to be healthy and making healthy choices signals the cells to modify themselves in such a way that they begin to return the physical frame to its optimal state of being.

For example, when the sun burns the skin, the body responds to the injury by increasing blood flow to the area, and healing begins immediately. However, at a cellular level, the injury's stress also modifies the cell's plans. The cells respond by producing melanin from the melanocytes in the skin, resulting in darker skin that will protect the body from future injury. Similarly, consciously changing the decisions you make about your body and the way you treat your body also makes your body's cells follow suit. Like the stress of the sun on the skin, consciously deciding to be healthy is an act of applying a stressor, an internal stressor, but a stressor nonetheless. This stressor, like any other stressor, will also work at the cellular level and, in the same way, stimulate the cells to create optimal health. Internal information received from you will pass through the nervous system and modify the cells' instructions so that the body will move toward its optimal state. Improving the decisions you make about your body consciously will cause the body's cells to improve along with you.

As soon as you are said to be born into this world, your perceived physical body begins to develop and change. Your perceived physical body develops from infant to child, child to teen, teen to adult, and adult to senior citizen. Despite all those changes over time, you, the awareness within, remain unchanged. You remain the captain of each new ship. While these physical changes cannot be avoided, their states of being can be managed. It is up to you to continually think about or imagine that you possess a healthy body and then decide to do all that is necessary to be and remain in that imagined state of health. Then, you will necessarily and naturally end up in your optimal state of health. Believing will lead to seeing.

Never compare your state of optimal health to others. The physical attributes you believe you possess are sufficient to exist peacefully in this perceived physical world. Your body's state of health is not like anyone else's. It is perfect for your specific life journey. Imagine that one human was given a free speed boat and another human a free barge. While both are boats, each was designed for these captains to manage very different journeys. The speed boat is tiny and can go incredibly fast but cannot carry cargo. The barge is a huge boat that can carry thousands of tons of cargo but cannot go very fast. It would be ridiculous to overload a little speed boat with tons of cargo or to try to race a gigantic barge against other small speed boats. Despite this, some human beings misunderstand the gift or fail to appreciate the qualities of the boat they possess. They become envious of the other boats or begin to believe that they were somehow cheated. Those human beings are consuming a poison called envy that will prevent them from achieving real and lasting peace until they voluntarily release it. Envy and doubt are internal conflicts that must be identified, released, and replaced with intellectual determination to become as healthy as one can be with the body that one believes one possesses.

LOVE YOUR NEIGHBOR

Humanity constantly appears to be going through interesting times. In today's world, political and social divisions are regularly highlighted by the news, social media, and political leadership in what could be understood to be covert attempts to sow hatred, mistrust, envy, and selfish ambition amongst the ignorant and poor masses. But times like this are nothing new. Humanity has been going through this since time immemorial. Since the beginning of societies, there have been government, social, and religious leaders who desired to gain control of their society. Once they gained control, they understood that the one who controls the information controls the minds of their subjects. They gain control of the minds of their subjects through political strategy, a kind of strategy wherein the leaders act publicly as two opposing parties that differ ideologically from one another on issues like poverty, immigration, taxation, and crime, which can never be solved, while privately maintaining solid, friendly relationships with others in the leadership class. For example, one side may publicly act in defense of the subject of crime, while the other side of the same group publicly opposes the subject, with both sides pretending to fight over crime in clear view of anyone who will watch, knowing crime can increase and decrease, but crime will never completely go away. One side of leadership will say we need fewer police, while the other side says we need more. One side will say we need more jails, while the other side says we need fewer. One side will say we need softer sentencing, while the other says we need harsher punishments. As these leaders pretend to argue over these kinds of issues, they involve the members of their community in such a way that the members of the community become divided, mistrustful, envious, and hateful toward one another until they eventually become eager to take sides openly. Once they have taken sides, they become willing pawns that ultimately take sides against their neighbors in exchange for favors, food, guns, and money from the leadership they believe is on their side. But what was the actual crime? The ignorance of the members within the community. The ignorance of the members of the community allows those in control to reach them and manipulate them, pitting neighbor against neighbor.

The politico-social environment in Judea, during the period that the Hebrews were subjected to Roman control, was likely no exception. What was the solution to this age-old problem back then? Knowledge. When the prophet Jesus recognized this problem among his neighbors in his own country, he was recorded educating his fellow citizens on the way to resist this kind of control and manipulation. In the King James Version of the New Testament, Jesus was asked what the greatest commandment was. Jesus responded that the first commandment was to love God with all your heart, and the second was to love your neighbor as yourself. In Mathew 22:37-39, Jesus stated, "Thou shalt love the Lord thy God with all thy heart, and with all thy soul, and with all thy mind, and the second is like unto it, thou shalt love thy neighbor as thyself." Then, Jesus told his followers just how vital these two commandments were. In Mathew 22:40, He stated, "On these two commandments hang all the law and the prophets." But what exactly did Jesus mean by these sayings? Let us unpack the logic.

Imagine looking out over the ocean. In your mind's eye, you see that the surface of the vast ocean is covered with waves. On the surface, the waves appear separate and distinct from the ocean, but in reality, they are separate and distinct in name and form only. If you could closely inspect each wave, you would soon discover that every wave has a form named wave, but each wave is composed of the same water as the ocean. The top of the wave is composed of ocean water, the middle of each wave is composed of ocean water, and the bottom of each wave is composed of ocean water. In fact, the entire form called "wave" is merely a temporary extension of the ocean. When the wave hits the shore, only the name and form of the wave are destroyed as the water within the wave simply returns to itself: the vast and unchanging ocean. Despite the form of the wave coming into and out of existence, the ocean neither loses nor gains a drop of its water. The ocean remains the one true reality.

It is like this with all of humanity. Like waves, all human beings appear as human beings in name and form, but their embodied soul, their awareness, is of the same vast unchanging ocean: God. In that respect, all conscious beings can be seen as infinite individual expressions or different aspects of God. Ocean waves take many different shapes, appear different from one another, and travel in many directions. If waves could think for themselves, one could imagine that the smaller waves might look up at the larger waves with jealousy.

Or the larger waves might look down on the smaller waves as if they were superior. One could imagine that the waves heading east might be angry at the waves heading in different directions. One could even imagine that most, if not all of the waves, would consider themselves very separate and distinct from all the other waves around them and that each of the waves might begin to make judgments about the other waves based primarily upon their preconceived notions about their different names and forms. All of these imaginary scenarios could be because of the wave's ignorance of their deeper connection, leading them to focus on the names and forms of one another rather than their actual common source. While concentrating on waves, they cannot see that they are all a part of the same ocean. It is similar with human beings. While humans may have different names and physical forms, they all share the same spiritual ocean of awareness within them, expressed as their consciousness.

When you look at the ones around you, you must use your intellect to remind yourself that your neighbors are also the children of God, expressions of God, just as you are. These human beings are not only your genetic relatives; they are connected to you spiritually. While they may be ignorant of their true nature right now, focusing solely on waves, their souls exist with your soul within the same spiritual ocean and are deserving of the same love, compassion, respect, and forgiveness as you.

Some say they were born again in the lord's spirit. Could they be expressing their newfound ability to see this spiritual connection? If one were to look at another as a part of the ocean of awareness instead of a wave, they would not be focusing on the color, height, weight, sex, nationality, religion, or political affiliation of the other person. They would instead be focused on the realization that they are each a part of the same thing, each a beautiful vessel full of the same ocean of awareness.

When children are small, they make mistakes and have accidents all of the time. It is easily understood that children make mistakes and have accidents because of their lack of knowledge. Supportive parents overlook all of that and can see the beauty within them. Regardless of their children's behavior, caring and supportive parents give their children love, compassion, respect, and forgiveness. They realize their children are only making these mistakes and having these accidents because they are too ignorant to understand how to behave appropriately in the world around them. Caring, supportive parents know that all of their children's mistakes and accidents are a normal part of their children's development, and these parents know their children will understand at the proper time. So, rather than trying to judge their children, hurt, condemn, or ostracize them, caring, supportive parents continually show endless love, compassion, and respect. They forgive their children and teach them the proper way after each misstep, regardless of how challenging or exasperating it can sometimes be for the parents. Caring, supportive parents do not love their children because the children are constantly being good. They love their children because they possess the power and ability to share their love with others regardless of how others behave.

It is the same with your neighbors. Those too ignorant to understand the truth of their nobility, the beauty of their true nature, or their interconnectedness with their fellow human beings will sometimes act like children, believing, like the waves, that they are separate from one another. Like small children, they may judge one another, be cruel to one another, be envious of one another, hate one another, and even hurt one another.

Some falsely believe that some people are good and others are bad. This is false because there is no such thing. Human beings are neither good nor bad. They are conscious beings that vacillate between good and bad behaviors depending on the moment, their ability or lack thereof, and how they choose to manage a situation. Those who make a good decision due to their knowledge appear good, and those who make the wrong decision due to ignorance appear bad. But the so-called bad ones learn from their mistakes, correct the behavior in the following situation, and then appear as good. Like the parent, you must intellectually see those who mis-behave as the ignorant children they are and show them love, com-passion, respect, and forgiveness, knowing that one day they will understand their mistakes were a normal part of their growth and development.

However, loving your neighbor does not require you to suffer on their behalf. If your neighbors are acting in a way that you believe is improper, show them love, compassion, and forgiveness, but do not make yourself responsible for or become involved in their poor choices. Do not enable their dysfunction. If you feel that they have become so lost or confused that they have become destructive, do not attempt to correct them or take on their challenges. Do not put yourself in any position that will take away your peace.

Differentiate between those who desire friendship and those who want control over you, and stay clear of those you believe seek to control you. Be kind, offer love, compassion, respect, and forgiveness, and share your knowledge when appropriate. But don't let them use you. Understand that no matter what you do for a person who seeks to control you, a person who seeks to use you, they will expect more and more until your life is no longer yours.

Loving your neighbor doesn't include prolonged contact with people who are negative, overly critical, repeat rumors, or are in a constant state of depression. Encourage, inspire, and share your knowledge with them when possible, but not at the expense of your peace. Some human beings are content with their suffering. That is what they have chosen and will continue to choose. Likewise, do not get involved if your neighbor is being envious, stealing, lying, cheating, or killing. Instead, remove yourself from that space as soon as possible.

Imagine the job of an ocean lifeguard. When the lifeguard sees someone drowning in the water, their first instinct is to take immediate action to render aid. However, the lifeguard is also trained to understand that some drowning victims will often unintentionally grab onto the lifeguard and drown the lifeguard while struggling to save themselves. So, as the lifeguard attempts to assist the drowning victims, they do so in a manner that will also protect them from potential harm. Like the lifeguard, follow your natural instincts and protect yourself from those you believe might destroy your peace. You deserve the same peace as any of the others.

It is easy to love your friends. It is easy to love those who love you in return. It is easy to love those who agree with you and those who help you. Like the exasperated parent, it can be difficult to love everyone as you would want to be loved regardless of their behavior. But despite your neighbor's conduct and your need for self-protection, you must intellectually remind yourself of their true nature and connection to you and forgive them of their trespasses as you would want to be forgiven.

To love your neighbor all the time, you must sometimes use your intellect to look deeper than the names and forms in front of you, especially when you believe they are misbehaving. Look at them from the perspective of your true nature, and visualize the "Ocean" within them. Show them love, compassion, respect, and forgiveness. If that approach feels too difficult, simply look at them and quietly tell yourself, "I do not love you because you are being good right now. I love you because I am." Your kindness will bless them and allow them to see the beauty of your true nature. It will also act as a mirror through which they can see their true nature more clearly. More importantly, loving your neighbor as yourself will bring you peace, create a more peaceful world, and be the binding that no political strategy or social manipulation can break.

CONTROL THE MIND

Your thoughts are yours, but they are not you, the awareness. Your thoughts are a product of your mind. Your brain cells gather and retain information from the outside world through your senses and make the information available to you as and when you desire. Each brain cell accepts and maintains a single piece of information from the external world. The information stored in these brain cells is a reflection of the external reality. When you review the information from your brain cells, the world you believe you see in your mind is not that reflection; it is merely your perception of the reflection. Your perception of the external world is different from the reality of the external world because of your sensory limitations and your mind's manipulation of the information received.

Imagine that your mind is a door-to-door salesperson, and you answered the door to your home to greet them. It is well known that door-to-door salespeople can be very aggressive; this salesperson is no exception. The salesperson in front of you is very self-assured and assertive. Almost immediately, the salesperson attempts to gain your confidence and prove that she is the only one capable of understanding your needs. The salesperson does her best to endear herself to you with her smile and kind words as she shows you her goods one at a time, optimistic that the item she is selling you is the one you need.

If you accept what the salesperson presents, you have made your choice. If you are not intellectually sure you want to choose what the salesperson is showing you, or a bit too much time has passed while you are thinking about what the salesperson is showing, the salesperson will quickly begin to show you other items. Very often, the salesperson will present things that have little or nothing to do with your actual desires. The salesperson may show you some lotions you were thinking about yesterday, a set of dishes, or the latest design in floor vacuums. The human mind is very much like the door-to-door salesman in this example.

When you begin to think about a subject, any subject, the mind immediately retrieves information stored in the neurons that it feels might be related to your query. Then it provides you the information with complete confidence that it has precisely what you need. Your mind presents options one at a time because the mind can only offer information stored in the brain cells one thought at a time. The mind can provide information so quickly at times that it can appear to you as a long train of thought. But despite appearance, the mind is limited in its ability to show one thought at a time. To visualize this, imagine that on a very dark night, you held onto a torch, lit the torch on fire, and began quickly swinging the lighted torch in a circle until there appeared to be a continuous circle of fire. You know that the torch only moves into different spots at different times as you swing it in a circle, but the torch moves so fast as you swing it that it gives the visual impression of a continuous circle of fire. It is like this with the mind. Even though one's thoughts may appear continuous, each thought is separate, so there is always space between each thought to change or stop a thought. Similarly, these individual thoughts can also be seen the way one sees bubbles in a fish tank. While watching the bubbles move upward from the bottom of the tank to the top of the water, it will appear as if there is one continuous stream of bubbles when, in actuality, there are millions of tiny individual bubbles. These individual bubbles of thought allow for interruption because a continuous thought cannot be interrupted.

This gives you incredible power. Once you understand the mind is yours but not you, you know that the mind is no more impressive than a door-to-door salesperson, and you understand it is you who has the ability and the authority to accept or reject whatever the mind offers as each thought is presented; you can appreciate that you are genuinely the mind's master. You have the power to change the way you think about the entire perceived external world because you have the power to change your mind. For example, if your mind randomly begins to think about something frightening, you may reject the item and require your mind to look at a different subject instead. If you are afraid of death and your mind randomly begins to explore any idea related to death, you can say something as simple as "I am hungry," and your mind will be forced to explore those new options related to your hunger. Rather than staying in the mental space the mind offers, even if only for a moment, require the mind to move onward to another subject and remind your mind that you are in control, not the mind. This will help you gain more control of your mind and give you more confidence in yourself.

It is essential to understand that the information from the external world you expose your brain cells to can be considered the total amount of information the door-to-door salesperson will have available to present to you. The mind can only collect options from that limited amount of information. Like the door-to-door salesperson, the mind is less impressive than it has been trying to convince you it is. With this knowledge, you may exercise your power over the mind and change your desires. You may desire to fill your mind with only positive items and as many as possible. This will change the kind of information stored by the mind and force the mind to offer more and more positive items each time a new thought or question arises. And if the mind offers any thought, and the idea is unwanted by you, your desire for anything else will force the mind to move onward as required. If you wish to stand, you have rejected sitting, and your mind must move with you as you stand. If you desire to eat, your mind must move with you as you explore food options. You are the master of your mind and not the other way around.

Some wrongly believe the best way to control the mind is to sit quietly alone in a space without distractions and attempt to remove all thoughts. They try to convince others that their version of meditation is a powerful tool that, if properly learned and performed correctly, will remove all negative or unwanted thoughts from one's mind. Sadly, removing all thoughts from the mind is impossible without being in a deep sleep, taking harmful drugs, being involved in a severe injury, or suffering from an illness that results in unconsciousness. The mind can only add and multiply thoughts; it cannot remove them. So, sitting and trying to remove a thought only makes you think of the thought more. Try NOT to think of a cat, and your mind will instantly add a picture of a cat. Try harder to remove the cat, and more cat-related ideas will appear. The more you try to make the thought go away, the more time you will spend thinking about the thought. The only cure is intentionally requiring the mind to add a different thought in its place, any thought you choose.

If your mind attempts to distract you from the thought you have chosen by placing other thoughts in front of you, consider the thought another unwanted item coming from the salesperson and require the salesperson to return its focus to whatever you want to see again. At first, you will only be able to control the salesperson for a few moments, but with practice over time, you will be able to train it to work in harmony with you throughout the entire day. Once you have trained the salesperson to remain in the space of your choice and focus on the thought of your choice, you have successfully controlled your salesperson, your mind. By requiring your mind to remain under your control, your mind will not be able to endlessly interrupt, distract, or offer unwanted items or items filled with prior misunderstandings and prejudices. You will be more at peace once you gain control of the mind.

BE CALM

Imagine sitting comfortably on the sofa and whiling away the time by petting a dog. The dog's name is unimportant to the story, but we will call the dog Max to ensure thoroughness. From your perspective, looking down on Max, you can see several fleas must have jumped onto the dog when it was outside in the backyard earlier that day. As you look more closely with your eyes squinted, you can just barely see amongst the fleas, two tiny fleas that appear as if they had just finished fighting. In what the two fleas convinced themselves was an epic struggle for power and control to determine who will become the dog's owner, one flea stands proudly with one foot upon his defeated opponent, and the defeated flea is lying flat on his back. The flea standing upon his opponent appears to be sure that this victory is his defining moment in life. The flea, lying flat on his back in defeat, appears to be sure that his loss is the most humiliating moment in his life. The victorious flea is elated and filled with joy, while the defeated flea is filled with sadness and depression. You laugh out loud a little as you look down on them because you know that neither of them is aware that they are merely two tiny fleas on a dog's back. The fleas cannot understand that the current event they find themselves in is only an incredibly small fraction of the grand scheme of things in the infinite manifest and unmanifest universe.

Sometimes, human beings can act like fleas on the dog's back. They allow themselves to be easily agitated or elated by momentary challenges, obstacles, and victories within the perceived physical world. They act as if the moment they are experiencing is an all-or-nothing moment. They allow their minds to trick them into believing that their entire lives depend upon the outcome. If these human beings could understand how infinitesimally small their daily perceived battles are compared to the infinite universe, they would see their similarity to the fleas. Even if they didn't laugh a little, they would likely feel much calmer.

Now, let us imagine drawing a line that was a single day long. Then, imagine drawing a line that is one hundred years long alongside the line that is a single day long. From the perspective of the one hundred years long line, the line that is a single day long will appear to be much smaller. Now imagine drawing a line that is one million years long alongside the line that is a single day long. From the perspective of the line that is a million years long, the line that is a single day long will appear as small or smaller than a tiny flea on a dog's back.

You, the awareness, are going to live forever. That means at some point in the future, the line of your life will be so grand that a line representing even a billion years will seem as small as a flea on a dog's back as viewed from outer space. Suppose you could train your mind to intellectually visualize your life more accurately in that way, as it truly is. In that case, you will better see how small the moment you believe you are currently experiencing is in the grand scheme of things. It will help you to become calm.

The manifest and unmanifest universe is infinite in scale. If you were to attempt to measure the two fleas against the infinite universe, the ratio would be so small that it would be more or less equal to zero. That is the perspective you should try to look at the perceived physical world from when you begin to feel the moment you are experiencing is intense, extreme, all-defining, or an all-or-nothing moment. That is the intellectual perspective from which you should continually train yourself to see the perceived physical world around you each time you feel you have achieved a great victory or have completely failed. Each of your successes, failures, errors, or good fortune are such small moments in time that they are also nearly equal to zero in the grand scheme of things.

The perceived physical world is a habitation that provides a temporary interactional medium you may experience in any way you choose. Your perceived successes and failures within the perceived physical world represent nothing more than a part of that. Each success or failure should be seen in that light. Remind yourself of this truth each day, and your perceived life will become much more manageable; you will be more kind to yourself, more forgiving of yourself and others, and much calmer.

If you find yourself terrified, agitated, angry, or feeling that the event you are experiencing is a defining moment in your life, you have merely, and thankfully, only temporarily, in most cases, lost control of your mind. Imagine that you are looking down an alley between two buildings on a dark and foggy night. As you look down the alley, a dark figure appears out of nowhere and seems to be moving closer. As the unknown figure approaches, it begins to take what you believe may be a human form, but you are unable to see precisely what is coming. This is when the mind starts to take control. The mind is like a monkey, and the possibilities are like branches on a tree that the monkey jumps to and from randomly. As you consider the possibilities of what might be approaching in front of you, the monkey begins jumping from branch to branch, covering all of the options in the tree. This is the problem. The monkey doesn't know that it should only jump to the branches that represent the more realistic possibilities. The monkey instead jumps to all of the branches it can in the time allowed. The more time allowed, the more branches the monkey jumps to and from. It offers everything from a dear friend to a terrible monster that will kill and eat you. If you allow the possibilities to agitate you, frighten you, drive you to anger, or believe the moment you are experiencing is an all-or-nothing moment, you have let go of your control of the mind. In these moments, it is imperative that you use your intellect to regain control of the mind. When the mind jumps to a branch and offers any specific possibility, you must run the information by your intellect to see if the possibility is even realistic. If the possibility seems unrealistic, simply prune the branch from the tree so the monkey cannot jump there again. Over time, your intellect will improve at pruning the tree, and you will be better able to manage new, frightening, or unfamiliar events as they occur in your perceived life. Training yourself to intellectually require your mind to visualize your challenges and obstacles more realistically will help you attain calmness.

Imagine storm clouds on the horizon. From where you are watching, the oncoming storm may appear terrifying. A long line of dark clouds covering the entire horizon, the distant rumble of thunder, the lightning coming and going in flashes that emanate from within the dark clouds, and a cool breeze moving from where you are watching, past you and towards the oncoming storm. It is easy to imagine the terrible possibilities of damage and destruction that might lie ahead. But when the wise see a storm cloud approaching on the horizon, they know that no matter how grand they imagine the coming storm will be, it will never be as bad as they imagined, and it will always pass in time. It will come into and out of their view like all their other life experiences. Similarly, if you really think about it, the storms that have come and gone in your life have sometimes seemed terrifying before their arrival and frightening as they passed. Still, the storms never actually turned out to be as bad as you imagined. And when the storms were reflected upon later in life by you, they often seemed as small as the battle of the fleas on the dog's back. Like the storm clouds that pass in the sky, so will all the other moments of this perceived existence. Their perceived intensity will diminish more and more over time as well. If you can practice looking at them from this perspective, you will become calm and be able to remain calm.

BE DETACHED

While sitting on the bank of a raging river after a significant rain storm upriver, a man and his family watched logs, broken branches, and debris float down the high water. As the man looked out towards the middle of the river, he noticed what appeared to be a beautiful black fur coat stuck to one of the floating logs. He pointed it out to his family, jumped into the river, and quickly swam towards the fur coat. Upon reaching the floating log and what he thought was a beautiful black fur coat, he realized it wasn't a black fur coat at all. It was a baby black bear. The baby black bear, afraid for its life in the turbulent water, grabbed the man tightly and held on. As the man and the bear struggled, the family yelled from the bank of the river, "Let go of the fur coat and come back; there is a log jam forming up ahead, and you will be crushed!" The man yelled back to his family, "I'm trying to let go of it, but it won't let go of me!"

This is attachment. Whatever you try to hold on to in life will also hold on to you. So, be very wary of what you desire. That beautiful car, great job, giant house, new boat, and all your other unnecessary desires will hold on to you and take away your peace. That beautiful car will require more maintenance, and parts are more expensive. That great job will require longer hours, more responsibility, and less time with family and friends. That giant house will have higher heating costs and cooling costs. The taxes will be higher, and there will be more to repair and maintain. And that boat. It is commonly known that there are only two good days of boat ownership. The day one buys the boat, and the day one sells the boat. Possessions like these will slowly eat away at your time and energy until you realize your life was not stolen away by those things; it was given away by your desires. Do not desire your neighbor's possessions, house, land, people in their life, or spouse. Remember, what may look like a beautiful fur coat from a distance may turn out to be, in reality, a real bear.

Instead, be like a peaceful employee of a large corporation. A person that looks very much like someone you may know. His dream has been to work for a large corporation, and he wants nothing more than to do his best at the job the large corporation gave him in return for a fair wage. From the onset of his employment, the employee decided not to concern himself with corporate matters, like whether or not the company was making a daily profit or whether the investors were getting good returns on their investments. The employee chose not to concern himself with any aspect of the corporation other than that which was explicitly in his job profile. The employee didn't get involved in office politics and didn't attempt to start any inappropriate office romances with any of the other employees or co-workers. The only thing the employee focused exclusively on during corporate business hours was his job. The peaceful employee had the wisdom to understand that he was separate and distinct from the company in every way except for the interaction required to perform the duties he was hired to perform. He decided to be responsible only for completing those duties, and in exchange for his service, the employee was given a handsome salary. The employee was content with the reward of his salary, and the corporation was content with his job performance.

While the peaceful employee was hard at work for the company, he made use of all of the material objects that the company made available to him. He understood that the materials and tools provided by the company were necessary to perform his job, and he was free to use them as and when needed to perform his duties. But the employee never desired to, nor ever attempted to take any of those things from his job home with him. The employee knew that taking the supplies away from the job site would not only be wrong but also pointless because the supplies are useless anywhere else but at his place of employment. The employee did his best with the materials available while remaining entirely unattached to the corporation, and the employee-employer relationship went along, year after year, very peacefully.

This perceived life is very similar. Your embodied soul exists within an interactional medium, a large corporation of sorts, filled with around 7 billion co-workers. Your job profile is to experience a perceived physical life, and you may experience it however you choose. If you can understand that the perceived physical world is yours but it is not you, that your embodied soul is experiencing it but, in reality, is separate from it, you will be able to live without attachment. Your payment will be the experiential knowledge that leads to peace. You have all the tools you will need to fulfill this job, and everything you will need in the future will become available as and when needed. All the materials you currently have and will gain over time are only useful during this perceived life. There is no reason to desire ownership of any material items because you cannot take any of the objects you have gained in this perceived life with you after this perceived life has ended.

To better understand this concept, imagine you are sitting comfortably on your couch playing a video game. You see the video game in graphic detail on the television screen, including your game character. You never believe, even momentarily, that the game character you see on the television screen is you. It is merely an imaginary image projected onto a television screen that allows you some needed entertainment and distraction. While you play the video game, you know that your avatar, your game character, will discover tools and objects in the video game that help you advance to the next level of the game. Still, you never believe you could take the tools or the objects away from the video game and put them somewhere else in your home. Even the idea of that would seem ridiculous.

It is similar in the perceived physical world. The tools and objects you use in this perceived life are useless anywhere else but within the game of this perceived life. Therefore, desiring to keep anything in the perceived physical world or take any of it to some location other than the perceived physical world should seem just as ridiculous.

This knowledge will help you to become detached in life, and that will lead to peace. You may choose to be like the employee who desires nothing but his salary or the gamer who desires nothing from the game but to enjoy the game. Approach each day and each challenge with a similar attitude. Remember that while the perceived physical world and all in it are yours to experience, the perceived physical world and all that is in it are not you, the awareness. Your soul is separate and distinct from the perceived physical world. You are not a physical being having a spiritual experience; you are a spiritual being having a physical experience.

Understand that your embodied soul will still exist long after the world you so deeply believe is real has gone from view. From that perspective, you will better see the perceived physical world as the temporary gift that it actually is. Desire only the salary of the experiential knowledge that leads to peace. Surround yourself with only the material items you need to play the game, but realize, like the tools in the video game, they are only temporary tools within the game that assist you as you interact with the perceived physical world and have no other value. Don't be selfish or try to horde anything in the perceived physical world. Use the material items of the perceived physical world as needed, and when there is no more need for the objects, share them or release them so that they may be helpful to others.

Like the clouds in the sky, all the material objects in the perceived physical world around you have come and gone. They were objects that were only useful for a time. The only thing that remains over time is you, the witness, yet you are not entirely the same. By integrating into and experiencing the perceived physical world around you, you have gained the knowledge necessary to manage the perceived physical world better. The knowledge you gain in the game of life is also a tool and can lead to a more peaceful experience. Knowledge and actions that lead to peace are of real value within the perceived physical world. That should be the object of your desire, like the employee's salary.

Non-attachment is not renunciation. Renunciation is the giving away of all one's possessions regardless of need, and it is the way of fools. Renunciation does not increase your ability to experience or enjoy the world. On the other hand, non-attachment only involves giving up one's mental attachment to the perceived physical world. It does not mean you let go of the perceived physical world or the objects within it. Non-attachment merely suggests that you should let go of your "prior misunderstanding" and realize that all of the objects of the material universe have always been, in reality, only the one God. Then there is nothing to see but God, nothing to hold onto but God, and nothing to desire but peace.

Almost all religions generally agree that God created everything from himself. If this is true, everything must be from God of God and in God. There is nothing but God. So, anything you see as other than God can be considered your mistake, your misunderstanding. When you can mentally understand or "see" this truth, you can use your intellect to instruct your mind to release its prior misunderstanding and create a new image you can now see with your mind's eye.

With this knowledge, you may let go of your prior misunderstanding about your children, "see" that each child is God, and enjoy your experience with God. You may let go of your misunderstanding about your husband or wife and "see" that they are also only God. You can then enjoy your experience with God. The more you let go of your prior misunderstanding about the material objects around you that you previously misunderstood and "see" that they are only God, the more peaceful you will become. In this way, you will naturally begin to let go of everything intellectually that you desired before and begin to desire to "see" the perceived physical world as it actually is. God is all around you and even within you. Jesus said, "Let those of you with eyes, 'see.'" If God is everything and is in everything, where else should we go to find him? If it initially seems complicated to "see" this simple truth, try to see only one thing as God. Then, when possible, add one item at a time. Since you will live forever, you should eventually be able to see God in everything within that time.

On a deeper level and in the proper time, once you fully understand the truth of who you are, you will also know that the entire perceived physical world has only existed as a projection within God. It is then that you will gently put down all of the remaining delusions you held on to before that moment.

BE SELFLESS

Most believe they will find peace and contentment if they can only accumulate many things for themselves. They are wrong. To see this, one only needs to look at the similarities between a billionaire and a beggar. The billionaire collects homes, planes, cars, clothes, and other random things. The beggar collects aluminum cans, bottles, clothes, twine, and other random things. They are both, in the end, collecting meaningless junk. It is only a matter of price that separates them in their minds. And when they are both considered dead, neither of them will be able to take any of their junk with them.

But then, how does one find peace and contentment? It can sometimes seem very elusive. Those who have not found peace or contentment cannot find it because they are searching for peace for selfish reasons. Those who have not found peace or contentment close their eyes and wonder where peace might be hidden. When they open their eyes, they ask how they might obtain peace for themselves. Those who have found peace and contentment close their eyes and recall moments when they helped others find peace. When they open their eyes, they ask themselves what they can continue to do to help others find peace. Those who find peace or contentment elusive cannot find it because they want God to give them what they are unwilling to give to others.

Let us look at the life of a peaceful and content man who, long ago, began his life in abject poverty. Armed with nothing but his will, he struggled throughout his youth until he achieved a higher education. He graduated, without any assistance whatsoever, in the top half of his class and was hired by a reputable company at a decent salary. After many years of selfless struggle, he deserved to put himself first. But shortly after that, he married a wonderful woman he learned had also come from humble beginnings and could not afford an education. So, rather than focus on himself, he put his wife first and used the money he earned from his reputable company to pay for her to become educated. Once educated, his wife was also hired into a reputable company at a good salary, and the couple decided to have children. They had two beautiful children. Rather than focus on themselves, the man and his new wife began to put their children first. The couple used their degrees, efforts, and newfound wealth to pay for their children's education in full. Many decades later, after the children also became successful, it would appear to some that the now much older man put himself last the entire time he was with his family, but that is not true. He chose to be selfless throughout his life and thus became the ladder that allowed each of his loved ones to climb to heaven, resulting in peace and contentment.

Or imagine a very poor but loving older sister who spent all her time and energy caring for her two younger siblings. The parents of the three children had sadly passed away only a few years earlier, leaving the children all alone. One hot afternoon, in their tiny one-room shack, the older sister noticed that the cupboard was bare, except for a single piece of bread. The older sister knew there was not enough bread for all three children. So, the older sister smiled, broke the bread into only two pieces, and gave each of the younger children as much as she could. Although the older sister was also hungry and could have quickly eaten the bread without the younger children ever finding out, her love and devotion to her younger siblings was greater than her desire. While it may appear to some that the older sister put herself last, she was, in reality, the first to make sure that her younger siblings were loved and cared for completely. This level of love and devotion is a true example of selflessness. Selfless people become like a funnel whenever they share the things they can live without with others. That which they give from themselves falls upon others like raindrops from heaven that fall more directly upon the world's flowers.

Selflessness is like a fireplace that draws cold air from the world and mixes it with the energy of its fire within to give back the radiant warmth of peace and contentment as the smoke rises safely out of the chimney. If God can be imagined as the spark that lights the fire of love and compassion within you, then a person's selfless devotion to others can be seen as the flame that peacefully warms the world. Be like the fireplace. Take the cold air from the world, heat it with your knowledge, love, kindness, and compassion, and release the energy within you outward into the world through your actions to warm the external world. Use the power of heaven within you to create heaven all around you while always desiring nothing but peace.

Anytime you receive blessings in life, use as much of it as possible to improve the world wherever you see it is needed. In doing so, you will create a flow of energy that draws more and more from the space known as heaven within you, and move it outward into the perceived physical world. The more you become determined to create heaven on earth for others, the more blessings from heaven will appear in size and frequency over time. These blessings will appear to others as good luck or good fortune, but they were, in fact, brought into the world by you.

But if you decide to take from the perceived external world, you will have reversed that flow of energy instead. Others will see this as selfishness. Selfishness has doubt as its source and always leads to suffering. Selfishness is an attempt by the mind to persuade the awareness into believing it should stop concerning itself with improving the perceived physical world and take whatever it can from the world in an effort to temporarily comfort the self. Selfishness is like closing the flume on the inside of a fireplace. Instead of the open flume allowing the fire to produce radiant warmth and release the smoke gently out of the chimney, the closed flume will prevent the smoke from going up and out of the chimney. With nowhere to go, the smoke will back up and fill the room with toxic smoke, causing everyone nearby to suffer. Selfishness, like the closed flume, effectively stops the natural flow of energy in the hypothetical fireplace that everyone could enjoy, and it leaves the one choking on the material objects they thought they desired. Feeling ever more empty, alone, and doubtful, they will either continue on the path of selfishness and their suffering will continue or allow the knowledge they gained from their suffering to change them for the better.

It should be easy to understand that if a person cannot see their connection to all humanity, it is natural to feel doubtful, alone, afraid, and then become selfish. Without truly understanding that all those around them are created from God, of God, in God, and are a part of God, they cannot see their actual connection to the much larger reality that they have never been alone, and there is nothing to fear. Imagine looking out over the ocean again to see this larger reality intellectually. You will see that the surface of the vast ocean is covered with waves. On the surface, the waves appear separate and distinct from the ocean, but in reality, they are separate in name and form only. If you could closely inspect each wave, you would soon discover that every wave has a form named wave, but each wave is composed of exactly the same water as the ocean. The top of the wave is composed of ocean water, the middle of the wave is composed of ocean water, and the bottom of the wave is composed of ocean water. In fact, the entire form called "wave" is merely a temporary appearance of the ocean. When the wave hits the shore, only the name and form of the wave are destroyed. The water within the wave simply returns to its true nature: the vast and unchanging ocean. Despite the name and form of the "wave" appearing to come into and out of existence, the ocean neither loses nor gains a drop of its water. The ocean remains the one true reality.

It is like this with all of humanity. Like waves, all human beings appear as human beings in name and form, but their embodied soul, their awareness, is of the same vast unchanging ocean: God. Reflect upon this knowledge as often as possible and use this knowledge to help you see your connection with all conscious beings. Then, use that knowledge to prioritize humanity with the same love and devotion the man gave to his family and the older sister gave to her younger siblings. By putting others' welfare before yours, you will never, in reality, be last. Instead, you have become the first to see the truth of the beauty of the world around you and the first to help others see a reflection of the heaven that has been all around them this entire time.

MAKE BETTER DECISIONS

Once, a great king felt cold in his tent, so he decided to go outside the tent to sit by a fire and get warm. As he walked out of the tent and towards the fire, one of his servants ran before him and placed a chair next to the fire for the king. As the King neared the fire, he noticed the smoke from the fire was blowing straight into the chair. He asked his servant, "Why did you put my chair directly in the path of the smoke?" The servant answered, "That is exactly the same spot where your chair was placed yesterday." This interplay reveals that one must not make decisions regarding possibilities in the future based on success in the past. One must make choices free from conflict or contradiction in the present moment. Decisions that worked in the past were affected by a specific set of realities that no longer exist in the present. Require your mind to change with the new circumstances you are confronting in the present moment to make a better decision. You can allow your mind to review information from the past to make a new decision. Reviewing past information is not the same as using past decisions.

Not so long ago, early one morning, a man sat comfortably in a donut shop and ordered a cup of tea and two donuts. The man smiled contently as he ate the donuts because they were delicious and quite filling. The man was so happy after that meal that he decided, from that day on, he would eat two donuts every day. After five years of eating two donuts daily, the man became seriously overweight. After five more years, the man developed diabetes and yet continued to eat two donuts every day. After five more years, his right foot became so damaged from diabetes that his lower leg had to be amputated. Despite this new reality, the man kept eating two doughnuts per day. His doctor finally asked the man why he wouldn't stop eating the doughnuts. The man said, "Once my mind is made up, I don't like to change it." This man is an example of someone who refuses to realize that a decision he made in the past was a mistake that he should have corrected as he received new information over time.

Just down the road in a town much like where you grew up was an older man sitting inside an auto mechanic shop watching a mechanic work on the engine of a four-wheel drive truck with nothing but a set of plastic children's tools. After the mechanic unsuccessfully tried to repair the engine for four hours, the older man asked the mechanic, "Why are you trying to fix the engine with plastic children's tools?" The mechanic answered, "They worked great when I was six years old." The mechanic could not fix the problem before him because he wanted his present moment to be the same as his past. He was living in a self-created illusion. The tools and ideas that were useful in his past were only helpful at that moment and only under the circumstances that existed then. They are of little to no use in a different moment. This reveals that the old tools that seemed to be perfect before must be released so you can focus on finding the proper tool to manage your situation in the current moment.

Some refuse to make decisions in the present moment and, instead, simply attempt to repeatedly re-use their old decisions from the past. Over time, as things gradually get worse, they often begin to blame whatever they can for their failures. This is not because they are mean or unkind. It is because they do not understand the importance of making decisions in the present moment. They will claim that their childhood was much better than today, their high school days were better than today, or if they are senior citizens, they will claim their adulthood was better than today. This illusion they created about their past being better than their present reveals an approximate date of when they stopped making decisions in the present moment and started making decisions that worked in the past as if running on autopilot.

When confronting the need to make any decision, if you refuse to change your mind as required under each new circumstance, it will likely end in a worse outcome, if not outright failure. These poor outcomes are only because you forgot the importance of making decisions in the present moment. Poor decisions usually involve attempting to create an outcome like the one that you remember from your past. But your past is an illusion created by you, and your future will never be the same as the past you so deeply believe was real. Your desire to have the same outcome today that you believe you had in the past will inevitably lead to a bad result. If you want your future to be like your past, you have forgotten all the reality surrounding your memory of that period. You do not recall the bad parts; you only remember the good parts. Just because you forgot the reality does not mean it wasn't there.

Take your time when confronted with any new decision. Do not allow anything or anyone to rush you. Be flexible enough to consider the possibilities. Do not use what worked in the past simply because it worked out well before. Instead, as each new situation arises, ask yourself five questions, "Will my decision help others? Will my decision hurt others? Is my decision beneficial for the world around me? Will my decision help me get to my dreams?" and most importantly, "Will my decision provide me with a sense of peace?" If your answers to those questions create peace within you, you are likely making the better decision.

ACHIEVE YOUR DREAMS

The perceived physical world can be likened to the most complex multiplayer video game ever built, constructed in such a way that your awareness exists within a three-dimensional medium that allows for interaction. This perceived life experience is yours to interact with and exist within. The names and forms that you believe you are currently facing in the game of life are the experiential aspects of the one true reality, God, and the internal world within your head is merely your perception of reality, what you have chosen to believe with your limited understanding. The external world can be considered the macrocosm, and the internal world inside your head can be regarded as the microcosm or the reflection of the perceived external world. For example, when you see a car on the side of the road, it does not actually go through your eye and into your brain before you can see it. What goes into your eye is merely the reflection of the light that shined upon the car. From there, your mind processes the information, combines it with the other prior information stored within the brain cells, and provides you with an image of the car. This miniature world exists only within your head and is influenced not only by the light you believe is coming in but also by the way in which your mind manipulates it and adds to it with the brain cells› prior stored information.

Understanding that the entire world you believe you are currently seeing and experiencing right now is in reality, merely complex images happening in your head, is essential because once you understand that the entire perceived physical world you believe you see is in your head, and it is you that is the owner of it, you will realize that you possess the power to change and rearrange the images. This understanding gives you incredible power because, with this understanding, you have the power to change the entire perceived physical world simply by changing how you think and act within the perceived physical world. The way to begin to change those images is to change your internal thought processes first. Begin changing your internal thought process by intellectually reminding yourself that you have the power and authority to create a peaceful world or to create suffering. Once established in that point of view, anything and everything you have ever dreamed of becomes possible over time.

With this authority, become intellectually responsible for your dream and decide to imagine any dream you believe would create that peaceful world. Visualize something that you feel would give your life meaning. Consider this to be your dream of the future. Then, use your intellect to create a clear picture of your dream and become determined to learn everything and do everything necessary to achieve that dream. That specific dream will become the intellectual framework upon which your future will be built.

Next, remove internal conflicts. As you create the picture of your dream, identify and remove any internal conflicts that would prevent you from reaching your dream, as these are simply the products of your doubts. This includes removing old habits or patterns of behavior that now conflict with your dream. For example, if your dream is as ambitious as ending world hunger or as simple as obtaining the food necessary to feed your family, and at the same time you desire a life relaxing by the pool, both cannot be achieved because the goals conflict with one another. This contradiction will keep both from being fulfilled. If your dream is to obtain the wealth necessary to provide for a family, but you do not want to do any work to obtain that wealth, or you attempt to become wealthy without integrity or through improper action, you will be poor. Likewise, if you believe that the rich are bad or evil, you have created a conflict within yourself that will prevent you from obtaining the wealth necessary to make your dream a reality until it is removed from you; by you.

Then, once you have intellectually removed all the internal conflicts you can imagine, take action. Become physically responsible for making the dream a reality as much or as little as you desire. Once you move the idea into action, your mind will begin to align with your intellect and help you find options and ways to adapt to and overcome the challenges that lay within the dream as they become apparent. In this way, your participation in the perceived physical world will allow for the discovery of solutions. These discoveries may come from anywhere, at any time, and will continue to come to you as long as you hold on to your dream.

As you take action to achieve your dream, you will notice over time that you are becoming, little by little, more successful at integrating into and adequately managing your perceived physical world. The more you focus on realizing your dream of creating a peaceful world, the more you will find solutions for the issues in your world. You will be, at that very moment, a human- "being" in that "you" are "being" responsible for your perceived world. It doesn't matter what you choose to become responsible for because, eventually, you will become capable of being responsible for it all over time. And remember, since you are going to live forever, there is no need to hurry, take shortcuts, sacrifice your integrity, or worry about how long it will take to get there.

Achieving your dream will be challenging. Accidents will happen, and mistakes will be made along the way. Do not be afraid to make mistakes or have accidents; they are a natural part of learning and development in the wondrous game of life. Greet each accident or error with a smile, and after you make the correction, gently let it go in the same way you would let go of anything else that no longer had any value or use for you.

Finally, with each dream realized, celebrate your ability to create the more peaceful world you imagined. Enjoy the reward of improved knowledge, peace, and contentment. Do not allow yourself to be distracted by those who will tell you that you haven't done enough or have done it the wrong way. Intellectually recognize that it is merely another attempt by your mind to convince you to surrender your faith. In those moments, use your faith and intellect to remind yourself that you are creating a more peaceful world in the perfect way and learning from the experience at the perfect pace. Each time you unselfishly create an even slightly more peaceful world, it is seen by all as a beautiful measure of your true inner nature.

THE END